Laugh and Cry Your Way to

Freedom

Changed Into His Image Through Inner Healing

by

John Chappell

Laugh and Cry Your Way to Freedom
Copyright © 2000 by John R. Chappell, III
ALL RIGHTS RESERVED

All Scripture references are from the Authorized King James Version of the Bible, unless otherwise noted. References marked NKJ are from the New King James Version of the Bible Copyright © 1979, 1980, 1982 by Thomas Nelson, Inc., Nashville, Tennessee.

The testimonies we have used as examples are based on actual events. Names of persons and places have been changed to ensure the privacy of the individuals involved.

Published by Serenity Books

ISBN 1-884369-97-9

Printed in the United States of America
For Worldwide Distribution

Books may be ordered directly from:

Rev. & Mrs. John Chappell
P.O.Box 172
Bartow, FL 33831
(863) 533-6656
JChap777@aol.com

Acknowledgments

This book would not have been possible without the rich heritage we received under the ministry of Wallace H. Heflin, Sr., his wife Edith Ward Heflin, and their amazing daughter Ruth Heflin, missionary to the world. I also learned much from Ruth's late brother, Wallace H. Heflin, Jr., particularly during our many overseas trips together.

The book came forth out of nearly twenty-five years of ministry to the inner healing needs of others, in partnership with my lovely wife Pattie. So much help, so many creative ideas and important editorial changes have come from my daughter Margaret. In the early years of the book's development, Bonnie Bailey graciously typed several inner healing tapes for me, and I am grateful for this help.

Pattie and I learned invaluable information on inner healing, particularly in connection with soul ties and fragmentation, from our friends Ron and Leon Watson of Charlestown, NSW, Australia. We are grateful to them also for setting up our itinerary in that country during 1991-1993.

I also gained much knowledge in the area of inner healing from many Christian authors, particularly from several books by John and Paula Sandford.

My thanks to the many other brothers and sisters in Christ who have greatly encouraged me and prayed for me through the years.

Contents

Introduction 7

1. Inner Healing: What Is It? 11
2. Inner Healing: Who Needs It? 18
3. The Baptism in the Holy Spirit and Inner Healing 32
4. Inner Healing Through Self-travail 45
5. Inner Healing Through Holy Laughter 52
6. Inner Healing Through Forgiveness of Others, Oneself and God 72
7. Breaking the Power of Generational Iniquity 89
8. Breaking the Power of Destructive Inner Vows 107
9. Negative Soul Ties, Idolatry and Fragmentation 115
10. The Renewed Mind and Inner Healing 133
11. Easy Steps to Life-Transforming Inner Healing (and Deliverance) 148

Appendix:
How to Receive the Baptism in the Holy Spirit 158

Introduction

Since 1973 my wife Pattie and I have been deeply involved in the inner healing ministry, a ministry of the Holy Spirit that produces a deep inner change (sanctification) within Christian believers so that we are progressively cleansed, healed within and conformed to the image of Christ. This ministry sets us free from various emotional and relationship problems that may have been caused by abuse, rejection or other crippling events of the past. We are enabled to receive deeply the forgiveness of God. We now can forgive ourselves. We are freed from unforgiveness toward others, toward God, and toward ourselves. This, in turn, frees us from bitterness and wrong attitudes so that we can become the loving individuals God has created us to be.

Over the past twenty-five years, we have seen the Lord Jesus, through the mighty power of the Holy Spirit, liberate thousands of Christians to walk in new intimacy with God. Life-transforming changes in their lives and joyful, fulfilling relationships with others have been the results.

Through these years of experience, this book has been birthed. The desire of my heart is to see you, the reader, and many others like you liberated in a similar fashion. I believe that you are not reading this book by chance. Some of you have exhausted every means for help. You have experienced one disaster after another in your life, and you are about to give up. God has the answer for you in this book. We have seen one "impossible" case after another set free by the Holy Spirit. This is a divine appointment, an answer to the cry of your heart to be changed, to be set free, so that you can walk *"in newness of life."*

Some of you may be reading this book because you have a desire to be more effective in setting others free from such spiritual hindrances. In either case, I believe your desire will be fulfilled.

A few years after becoming involved in the inner healing ministry, I found, to my surprise, that almost all Christians were oppressed to some extent by evil spirits, and some to a great extent. We thank God for using us to help Christians be delivered from such oppressions.

I am not suggesting that these people were demon possessed. As born-again Christians, we cannot be demon-possessed or have an evil spirit abiding within our own spirits. We can, however, be oppressed by evil spirits in our souls (the realm of our natural emotions, mind and will) and, as a result, need to be set free. In most cases, such oppression results from having some form of sin in our lives or from having been sinned against. Repentance, forgiveness of others, or both are usually essential keys to deliverance.

This ministry has changed my own life. I have been astonished at the dimension of pride, rebellion, deception, jealousy, unforgiveness, rage, unbelief and other areas of darkness the Spirit has helped me to overcome through the years. God has made one change after another in my life, and through His grace, I now have peace within and walk in a dimension of intimacy with the Lord Jesus that I feel compelled to share with others.

The Christian life is meant to be beautiful and exciting, and although we are all far from perfect, the Lord is ready to make many much-needed changes in us. When we are changed, then we have a responsibility through the Holy Spirit to help change others.

In the pages of this book, I want to share with you some of the simple, yet life-changing, truths that have turned my life and the lives of thousands around. I know that as you cooperate with the Holy Spirit and hunger to be changed, the knowledge in this book will revolutionize your life as well. God loves you and has a plan for you to be *Changed Into His Image Through Inner Healing*.

In our own ministry, we have found that we can minister inner healing and deliverance in several different ways. Sometimes it is by mass prayer for a large group of people, and many lives have been changed this way. Whenever possible, however, we give special attention to each individual, and this is usually even more effective. While we would welcome the opportunity of praying with each of you who read this book, inner healing comes from the Lord, so you can be healed as you read and put into practice what you learn.

You can be set free from the hurts, rejections and heartache of the past without anyone else praying for you. You will discover how — through some simple, Holy Spirit-inspired methods or principles — you can be released from rage, lust, depression and fear and from being a victim or a victimizer of others. You can have victory in all of these areas because the Word of God states clearly:

In all these things we are more than conquerors through him that loved us.   Romans 8:37

It is my hope that this book will be used to raise up and equip teachers who will have inner healing/deliverance ministries and who, in turn, will teach others to have similar ministries. In this way the entire Body of Christian believers throughout the world will be benefitted.

When I use the expression "inner healing" in this book, my intention will always be to include deliverance from evil spirits. The two ministries are different, but they are intertwined; they work together. Inner healing is usually needed for deliverance to be lasting. Although much deliverance will occur automatically when one experiences inner healing, there are many occasions when specific, powerful prayer is needed for complete deliverance.

The principles and methods you read about in this book are scriptural and Holy Spirit-inspired, and they have set thousands free. We have used all of them over a period of many years, so we know they work. Use them to be set free yourself and to help free others. Let them be tools for the glory of God and for the upbuilding of His Kingdom.

Now, turn to Chapter 1 and see what exciting things the Lord has in store for you.

John Chappell
Bartow, Florida

Chapter 1

Inner Healing: What Is It?

The Spirit of the Lord is upon me, because he hath anointed me to preach the gospel to the poor; he hath sent me to heal the brokenhearted, to preach deliverance to the captives, and recovering of sight to the blind, to set at liberty them that are bruised.

Luke 4:18

He healeth the broken in heart, and bindeth up their wounds. Psalm 147:3

Man has three parts: body, soul and spirit. It is our spirits that are reborn at salvation. When we invite Jesus to come into our hearts, we are born again, made *"new creatures"* in Christ. Our spirit, which was dead in sin, becomes alive in God. We are now one spirit with the Lord (see 1 Corinthians 6:17).

There is more to us, however. We human beings are complex creatures. We possess a soul (the realm of the emotions, mind and will), and we live in a body. It is within the soul realm that we find things that are still displeasing to God: pride, rebellion, fear, lust, unbelief, unforgiveness, rage, jealousy, emotional pain, rejection and many other areas of darkness. A vast amount of inner healing is needed to achieve the abundant, victorious life God has promised to each of us.

Some call the ministry of inner healing "soul healing" because it is healing that takes place in the soul of a person, primarily in the emotions. Jesus came to set men free, and He does it through inner healing.

Some call the inner healing ministry simply "restoration" because it involves a restoring, or making new, of the soul. As David said, *"He restoreth my soul"* (Psalm 23:3). God is still in the restoration business.

Others call this ministry "the healing of memories" because the emotional pains and poisons from old memories are removed through inner healing.

Still others call this ministry "death and rebirth" because it is, in fact, an appropriation of Christ's death and resurrection for us. As Saint Paul declared in Galatians 2:20, *"I am crucified with Christ: nevertheless I live."* His life in us frees us from destructive influences.

By any name, this ministry involves a healing of the inner man, distinguishing it from outward or physical healing, the healing of the body. It is the healing of emotional, mental and physical abuse, usually inflicted in the early years of our lives by parents or other family members or friends.

All of us have buried anger, resentment and even rage within us, which began building up in early childhood.

Inner Healing: What Is It?

Usually this anger builds up over the years until it eventually reaches the boiling point. The degree of unhealed hurts, anger and rage is incredibly great even in those of us who had "good" childhoods.

Common problems that we face include self-hatred, fear, inferiority feelings, depression, anxieties, critical thoughts and anger. These often lead to compulsions such as pornography, sexual lust, overeating, drug use and alcoholism.

The good news is that we can be set free by touching the hem of Jesus' garment. A new life awaits us. Some people have been suffering for ten or fifteen years or longer without knowing that there is hope. Some have been tormented for twenty or thirty years or longer. It is time for them to be set free.

Jesus Ministered Inner Healing

Through His shed blood, Jesus has purchased for us a perfect, complete plan of salvation. Peter wrote to the churches:

> *According as his divine power hath given unto us ALL THINGS that pertain unto life and godliness, through the knowledge of him that hath called us to glory and virtue.* 2 Peter 1:3

The *"all things"* here includes not only forgiveness for our sins and healing of our bodies, but also the healing of our sorrows and other emotional hurts. As Isaiah foretold:

> *Surely he hath borne our griefs, and carried our sorrows.* Isaiah 53:4

Inner healing also includes deliverance from evil spirits and from the curses of generational iniquity. Jesus became a curse for us, and we must learn how to receive, to appropriate, all that He has provided for us.

Of Jesus, it was said:

> *How God anointed Jesus of Nazareth with the Holy Ghost and with power: who went about doing good, and healing all that were oppressed of the devil.*
> Acts 10:38

This is what Jesus did. This is why He came. His divine mission was *"to heal the brokenhearted,"* *"to preach deliverance to the captives,"* *"to set at liberty them that are bruised."* All of the other benefits of Jesus' ministry are still available to believers today, and the same is true of inner healing. As I minister deliverance from oppression and pray for people to be healed of its root cause, what I see Jesus doing in the life of believers today is life-changing. This ministry was valid in Jesus' day, and it is still valid today.

What Healing Do We Need?

What is it that we need to be healed of? Primarily it is rejection or other types of serious abuse by key people in our childhood. Abuse, particularly that committed by mother or father, is the root cause of almost all of our emotional and relational problems. These include problems with a marriage partner, children, friends, fellow church members and fellow workers. Most people are not aware

Inner Healing: What Is It?

that even while a baby is in its mother's womb, life-damaging hurts can begin. Yes, even before birth, babies can sense that they are being rejected, that they are not wanted by Mom or Dad. This is emotional abuse and requires much healing in later life.

If you find it difficult to hug your children or to frequently tell them that you love them, or you feel uncomfortable when somebody compliments you or wants to hug you, this may be an indication that you need to be set free from bondages developed in childhood. Rejection and a lack of unconditional love have left scars on many of us.

Some people are married and they still don't feel comfortable touching and being touched. How can this be? These people need God's healing touch on their souls.

Some people can't say the simple words "I love you." They cringe when they try to say it. That's not normal, and it requires healing.

Some people cannot understand how to relate to their children, to their spouse or to their co-workers. Some can't maintain any relationships in their lives. They desperately need the healing Balm of Gilead.

Many Christians have low opinions of themselves, carried over from childhood. But God wants us to see ourselves as He sees us — unique, precious and worthy of compliments. He loves us just as we are — unconditionally. We can't earn His love, and we can't lose it either.

You and I were created to have an intimate love relationship with God through our Savior, Jesus Christ. It is coming to "know" God and learning to trust Him, becoming totally dependent on Him, that gives meaning to life itself. From that perfect unity of our soul and spirit with God, we are enabled to live our lives in godly relationships with our loved ones and with others.

Because of the fall of man, however, because of Adamic sin, everything that God created in this world has, to a large extent, been corrupted or defiled. We are born in this world with the Adamic, sinful nature. It is only through God's grace, through the merit of the shed blood of Jesus, that we can be made clean and whole again. And once we know Him, He desires to remove anything that still hinders our intimate relationship with Him.

When we come before God in prayer, He looks forward to it just as much as we do. It is a special time for Him to enjoy our presence. It is His opportunity to show us His love. He delights in talking to us and in listening to us talk to Him. He longs for this fellowship, and misses it when we do not take time for Him. Nothing must be allowed to stand between us and God, and if the hurts of the past are keeping us from His best, it is time for His healing.

Conclusion

In conclusion, inner healing is a ministry of the Spirit intended for use in the Church today to bring us into a closer relationship with the Lord Jesus Christ and to make us more like Him. The Lord is still transforming my own life through inner healing, and I am so grateful to Him for this blessing.

If you will determine to be changed and will cooperate with the Lord, He will bring you the deep inner healing

Inner Healing: What Is It?

you so desperately seek. He desires to set you free to be the real you, free to give love, to receive love, and to be more than a conqueror in every area of your life. He is calling you to *Laugh and Cry Your Way to Freedom* and be *Changed Into His Image Through Inner Healing*.

Chapter 2

Inner Healing: Who Needs It?

Surely he hath borne our griefs, and carried our sorrows ... . He was wounded for our transgressions, he was bruised for our iniquities: the chastisement of our peace was upon him; and with his stripes we are healed.   Isaiah 53:4-5

As we have seen, *"griefs"* and *"sorrows,"* especially the ones suffered in our childhood years, damage us emotionally and can prevent us from becoming the people God has created us to be. The bad fruit that develops from these childhood hurts includes unforgiveness, bitterness, insecurity, wrong attitudes, sexual sins and various emotional problems. In the atonement, Jesus has taken these deep hurts, sorrows and griefs of the past and has purchased both physical and inner healing for us through His shed blood. The purpose of the inner healing ministry is to set us free from the results of such abuse and rejection and to enable us to enjoy fulfilling, victorious lives. Through inner

Inner Healing: Who Needs It?

healing, we are liberated from being victims of the past, and are able to become *"more than conquerors"* in Christ.

From God's dealings in my own life, and from our experience in ministering to thousands of Christians for more than two decades, Pattie and I have learned many new things about the inner healing ministry. What we have found in the Body of Christ in general has surprised us.

All of Us Need Inner Healing

All of us need a great deal of inner healing. Wounded and hurting Christians need far more inner healing than I originally believed necessary. Many Christians have a reservoir of unhealed hurts and hidden rage. This may even include those who have already received much inner healing. All of us need to know how to receive inner healing and deliverance on a continuing basis. This is a lifetime undertaking, part of the continual work of inner sanctification, of the process of being conformed to the image of Christ.

Pastors, deacons and even well-known Christian leaders fall into sexual and financial sins (and it happens everywhere in the world and in every denomination). Many of them desperately desire help, but they don't know where to go to get that help. It is surprising how many Christian leaders don't even know that inner healing exists.

Living in Denial

Others who know about the inner healing ministry but

refuse to seek it for themselves are simply denying that they need help. The truth is that few of us want to face our need for such healing and perhaps even deliverance. We prefer to hide from God and from ourselves. The very thought of being needy can be frightening to us. We like to feel that we pretty much "have it together" and are in control of our lives. The denied problems of rejection, insecurity, rage, lust, depression, self-hatred, dishonesty and addictions therefore go underground, only to surface later in destructive ways.

Such denial can eventually lead to emotional ruin of various kinds: broken marriages, deeply wounded children and destroyed ministries. Jesus is ready to set us free from all emotional hang-ups and paralyzing memories of the past.

What does it mean when we say that people are "living in denial"? It means that they are unwilling to face the painful truth about themselves or that they are minimizing serious problems. The refusal to acknowledge a serious drinking habit, an out-of-control eating habit or a sinful thought-life are common examples of denial. Not wanting to admit that we have a bad attitude, negativity, self-righteousness or pride are others. We consider our criticism of others as righteous indignation, not sinful judging. We refuse to see that we have a serious problem with unforgiveness, with jealousy, or with selfishness. We deny that our problems are being caused by us. We blame others, circumstances, our parents and even God, but refuse to accept any responsibility ourselves.

I am speaking from experience, for I have been guilty of much of the above. We are all guilty of this, and usually

Inner Healing: Who Needs It?

to a great degree. It is our nature to deny our need. The Bible declares:

> *The heart is deceitful above all things, and desperately wicked: who can know it?* Jeremiah 17:9

None of us can know his own heart without a revelation from the Holy Spirit. The Lord is willing and eager to show us our hearts, but we must cooperate with Him. He will reveal to us the dark areas, the sins, the negative mindsets, the traditions of man, and the weaknesses that need to be cleansed, changed and removed. He tells us:

> *I the LORD search the heart, I try the reins, even to give every man according to his ways, and according to the fruit of his doings.* Jeremiah 17:10

I can teach on denial because I experienced it. It took me many years to be able to admit the painful truth that my father never told me he loved me and seldom hugged me. Since then, I have spent hours in prayer being freed from this painful rejection. With the inner healing I experienced as a result, I have moved into a whole new place of peace and joy, and I have developed a more intimate relationship with God and with others.

My Extensive Anger List

Some years ago while I was teaching about the enormous amount of unforgiveness and buried anger every person has, God gave me a surprising revelation. Like most

Christians, I thought I had already forgiven everyone. I was sure that hidden anger was no problem in my own life. The Spirit of God, however, had a different idea about how anger-free I was. He showed me twenty-one different people against whom I still had unforgiveness and resentment. Some of this resentment went back twenty to forty years. I had mentally forgiven most of these people, but God requires heart forgiveness.

When the Lord revealed this, I had a long prayer session, and one by one God set me free from my unforgiveness toward each of the twenty-one people. This experience brought a wonderful new peace into my life. We all need inner healing.

The Prevalent Spirit of Lust

To my astonishment, I have found that anywhere from seventy-five to ninety-five percent of all Christian men and perhaps as many as fifty percent of all Christian women need deliverance from the evil spirit of lust. Such spirits attack the thought-life of the believer and often lead them into pornography and other forms of immorality.

Once when I was teaching a Sunday school class of thirty born-again Christian men, twenty-seven of them confessed to having a substantial problem with lustful thoughts, and three or four of them confessed that these lustful thoughts plagued them throughout the day everyday. Only one or two of those men knew how to get victory.

Inner Healing: Who Needs It?

In a marriage seminar that we held, eight of the ten men present expressed their need for deliverance from a spirit of lust.

In both of these groups, the men repented and asked God to deliver them. I prayed for them, and they were set free from lust. They reported feeling a great change within, and it became much easier to avoid lustful thoughts after that.

In an overseas meeting that Pattie and I conducted, fifteen pastors and leaders expressed a desire for deliverance from a spirit of lust. These pastors repented, and through the power of the Holy Spirit, God delivered each one of them.

We Must Change

We usually blame others and outward circumstances for the difficulties and disappointments in our lives and even for our personal failures. We must be courageous and recognize that we are the ones who need to change, not others. We are called to be more than conquerors through Christ Jesus, and it is inward change — being conformed to the image of Christ — that will lead us to a life of victory and joy. If we continue to deny the truth of our need to change, we prevent God from transforming us into His image. We reject the very thing that will bring healing and fulfillment into our lives.

Even if you have received much inner healing and deliverance from the Lord, you almost certainly need much more. Here are some signs indicating such need:

Laugh and Cry Your Way to Freedom

1. You were not hugged, cuddled, embraced or told verbally that you were loved by one or both of your parents.
2. As a child, you were abused mentally, emotionally or sexually. This includes abuse through religious legalism. It also includes having to earn love and not receiving it unconditionally.
3. You had a one-parent family, alcoholic parent(s) or the divorce of your parents during your childhood.
4. You have had a painful teenage period or marriage(s.)
5. You have one or more compulsions or addictions to things such as alcohol, drugs, food, gambling, work, sexual fantasies, rage, soap operas or overspending.
6. You have many negative, critical, jealous or fearful thoughts, or you have a habit of boasting or putting others down verbally.
7. You have many lustful thoughts or habits.
8. You have undergone one or more abortions.
9. You experience rebellion against authority figures.
10. You suffer from constant marital problems.
11. You experience much stress in your life.
12. You easily lose your temper with loved ones (or others). This may be the tip of the iceberg of much underlying pain, fear, rage and insecurity.
13. You experience feelings of inferiority, depression or sadness. Also, there is a lack of peace and joy in your life.

Inner Healing: Who Needs It?

14. You exhibit dishonesty, lying or exaggeration.
15. You were involved in the occult before salvation. Even if you have had much deliverance, you will need not only more deliverance, but also inner healing, cleansing and, probably, further breaking of the generational curse of occultism.

If any of these sound like you, God wants to heal you on the inside — to change you, to set you free. Be courageous, and come out of your hiding. Be determined to leave your state of denial and face truth so that God might set you free in deep and mighty ways.

Did You Really Have a Good Childhood?

You may insist that you had a perfectly wonderful childhood, but tell me, "How often did your father hug you? How often did he sit you on his lap and tell you he loved you? The answer in my own life, and perhaps in yours as well, is "never" or "not very often."

How about your mother? Did she hug you or tell you she loved you often? You answer may be, "We just weren't that kind of family!" A lack of hearing those heartfelt words "I love you" and experiencing frequent hugs and kisses from your parents has had a tremendous negative effect on your life whether you have realized this before or not.

Because your parents provided you food and clothing, and they didn't abuse you physically, you may have thought you had a good childhood. However, if you were not hugged and frequently told you were loved, there is a great emotional wound within you, an emotional vacuum. This causes suppressed emotions and inner rage. You need to be healed from this wound and delivered from the rage within. Jesus will fill up that empty place in your heart with His love.

The Trauma of the Teen Years and Its Aftermath

The teenage period is a time of questioning and experimentation. During this time, many young people investigate the supernatural. Unfortunately, it is usually the occult instead of the supernatural working of the Holy Spirit, as most teens are not aware that godly supernatural gifts even exist. Many teenagers get involved with Eastern religions, use ouija boards, study horoscopes and astrology, have seances or visit palm readers. Such involvement opens these young people up to evil spirits that can plague them for the rest of their lives unless they are deeply ministered to through inner healing and deliverance.

During the teenage years, people make many wrong choices, and this brings about trauma and emotional pain from which some never fully recover. When teenagers experiment with sex, they forge a negative bonding to their sex partners, damage their emotions and harden their conscience to sin. Their hearts are fragmented and torn. Such sexual experiences negatively influence a person's thought-life.

If this describes you, and you are now married, most likely it has been difficult for you to bond deeply with your marriage partner. The more sexual affairs you had in the

Inner Healing: Who Needs It?

past, the harder it is for you to have the close bonding desired with your spouse. It is like a piece of adhesive tape: each time you use it, it loses some of its ability to stick. When you lose your ability to stick emotionally to our marriage partner, you subconsciously find yourselves looking around for others to love. The soul ties that develop from these premarital sexual partners need to be broken, your damaged, fragmented soul needs to be healed, and you need to be set free from guilt feelings and shame.

The Bible tells us that "two become one" in marriage. In the sexual relationship, married or not, you become one with your partner. During sexual union, evil spirits from one partner are transferred to the other. We need deliverance from these evil spirits.

Damage From Extended Grief Over the Death of Loved Ones

The death of key people in your life results in deep emotional pain. When a loved one dies, our society discourages us from properly grieving. Tears of grief, that might normally continue for weeks or even months, bother those around us. Yet such tears (unless carried on for too long) are necessary for our mental and emotional health. The vast majority of us have not cried nearly enough for the death of our loved ones. Therefore, much of the grief and emotional pain remains. This produces many negative side effects in your life, including stress, arthritis, hidden resentment, depression and even negative soul ties with your deceased loved ones.

Damage From Verbal Abuse in Childhood

When we were small children, we believed whatever our parents told us. They were like God to us. Children are wounded deeply when their parents speak negative words like "You're stupid," "You're no good," or "You will never amount to much." Those negative words become established in one's heart and become a curse upon one's life. If the curse of such words is not broken, it will hinder you greatly throughout the entire course of your life.

At first, you may be succeeding at your job, in your business, in your marriage, or in your ministry, but for some reason you repeatedly do something that causes you to fail. This curse needs to be broken through inner healing and deliverance. As we shall see, you also need to start substituting words of faith for the negative statements that have dominated your life until now. Your mind must be changed, renewed by the Word of God, changed to see things the way God sees them.

Damage From Sexual Abuse in Childhood

Abuse can be mental, emotional or physical. Statistics show that about one out of four girls and a high percentage of boys under the age of ten have been abused sexually. The abuse is usually carried out by one of their own family members, a friend of the family, or a neighbor. As they become adults, those who have suffered such abuse critically need inner healing if they are to be free to function as emotionally healthy adults.

Inner Healing: Who Needs It?

Sexual abuse marks one as a victim and, like a powerful magnet, draws further abuse into one's life. A girl who has been sexually abused in the early years will often be abused or even raped as a teenager. There seems to be a sign over such children identifying them as potential victims. This can be explained. Through the process of transference from the abuser, this child has received a seducing spirit and a spirit of lust. He or she is usually unaware of having such a spirit, but this evil spirit draws, or seduces, abusers or rapists.

Let us put names to some of these needs in order to personalize the need for inner healing:

Anne: Sexually Abused by Her Brothers

Anne was sexually abused by her two brothers when she was a child, and she was raped in her early teen years. Then she went through two physically abusive marriages. As Pattie and I ministered inner healing to her, she sobbed deeply. We broke the soul ties with her abusers and prayed deliverance over her from various spirits.

She was able to deeply forgive her two brothers and her two ex-husbands for the first time. There was a marvelous change in her life. All bitterness, shame and self-pity departed. She glowed all over, filled with the peace and love of God. This is what the Lord does for His children through inner healing, and He will do it for you too.

Fred: Unloved by His Parents

Fred was raised on a dairy farm. He had good, moral, hard-working parents, who provided him with a stable home, delicious farm-cooked meals, fine clothing and a good education. He thought he had a near-perfect childhood and didn't understand why his emotions were so imprisoned, so suppressed. This is typical of many of us. Fred had suffered, as so many have, the childhood abuse of not having been held in his parents' arms and of not having been verbally told he was loved.

As we ministered inner healing to Fred, one by one his emotional walls began to crumble, and his suppressed emotions, including rage, began to be released. He was able to forgive his parents, and he began to come alive. You may need the same release.

Helen: Traumatized by Her Husband's Infidelity

Eight years previously, Helen's husband had torn her heart through an affair with another woman. He had sincerely and deeply repented, and it was apparent that he loved Helen, and she loved him. She tried to forgive him again and again, but her pain was so deep that when they would come together in the marriage bed, she could not bring herself to give herself physically to him. "Will you pray for me," she pleaded, "to be set free from those thoughts of what my husband did eight years ago so that I can have a normal marriage?"

I got ready to lay my hands on her head, but the Holy Spirit stopped me. "Don't pray for the relationship with her husband now," the Lord showed me. "Pray for Helen's relationship with her father, for that is the root of the problem."

I prayed for Helen to be healed of the deep hurts she

Inner Healing: Who Needs It?

had suffered through her father's rejection. She was able to fully forgive him, to appreciate him, even to love him. Having been set free of unforgiveness toward her father, she was then able to deeply forgive her husband for his unfaithfulness, and her marriage was healed. From that day, Helen was also free to love and trust her husband, and even to trust God more deeply. When she and her husband left, they looked like honeymooners.

Conclusion

Any person who has marriage problems, insecurity, rage, lust, depression, stress, self-hatred, fears, negativity, dishonesty or addictions is in need of inner healing and/or deliverance. Preachers and evangelists who desire to preach with brokenness and compassion are in need of inner healing and/or deliverance. All those who desire to be more intimate with God and more intimate, vulnerable and transparent with their loved ones and with others are in need of inner healing and/or deliverance. I need it; you need it; we all need it.

The chapters that follow will reveal how easily and quickly you can receive inner healing and, through it, become the person God has created you to be. I challenge you to *Laugh and Cry Your Way to Freedom* and be *Changed Into His Image Through Inner Healing.*

Chapter 3

The Baptism in the Holy Spirit and Inner Healing

But ye shall receive power, after that the Holy Ghost is come upon you.   Acts 1:8

And when the day of Pentecost was fully come ... they were all filled with the Holy Ghost, and began to speak with other tongues, as the Spirit gave them utterance. ... and the same day there were added unto them about three thousand souls.   Acts 2:1-4 and 41

Forty days after His resurrection, Jesus ascended to Heaven. On that momentous day, He commanded His disciples: *"Tarry [wait] ye in the city of Jerusalem, until ye be endued with power from on high"* (Luke 24:49). After Jesus had gone, the disciples returned to Jerusalem and went into an upper room. About ten days later, on the Jewish feast day of Pentecost, about one hundred and twenty of the disciples, including Mary the mother of Jesus, were baptized in the Holy Spirit in that upper room. The Holy

The Baptism in the Holy Spirit and Inner Healing

Spirit came into that room like a mighty, powerful wind. At the same time, purifying, sanctifying tongues of fire came upon them, and they all spoke in other tongues. It was a life-transforming experience of great power and inner change.

In the Bible, the infilling of the Holy Spirit always appears to have been accompanied by two things — by a mighty inner transformation and by speaking in other tongues. On the Day of Pentecost, all those who received spoke in other tongues. Paul spoke in other tongues when he received the baptism of the Spirit in Damascus. When those who had gathered at the house of Cornelius in Caesarea were filled with the Holy Spirit, they also spoke in tongues (see Acts 10:46). When the Apostle Paul laid hands on the disciples of John the Baptist at Ephesus, they were baptized in the Holy Spirit, *"and they spake with tongues, and prophesied"* (Acts 19:6).

The baptism in the Holy Spirit with speaking in other tongues is the key to a deeper prayer life and to a more intimate relationship with the Lord Jesus. The Word of God comes alive when it is quickened to you by the Spirit, you are able to hear the voice of God more easily, and visions come to you more freely. We should get our children filled with the Spirit at an early age. One of ours was filled at age five, one at six, and one at ten. Because of this, all of them began hearing the voice of God and having visions while they were very young.

The baptism in the Holy Spirit immediately gives you a greater anointing to minister to others, whether it is in preaching, teaching, singing, witnessing, praying for the sick or delivering the oppressed. So the sooner you can receive it, the better.

Laugh and Cry Your Way to Freedom

New converts and millions of Christians in every denomination and in every nation are receiving the baptism in the Holy Spirit and speaking in other tongues. Recent estimates are that there are 240 million Spirit-filled believers worldwide. This experience brings more power, joy and a greater love for Jesus into the lives of all those who receive it.

Our Personal Day of Pentecost

The same night that Pattie and I received Jesus into our hearts we were baptized in the Holy Spirit, and both of us spoke in tongues. Pattie spoke in three different languages. She also had several visions, received words of knowledge about friends of ours, and felt the arms of Jesus go around her. She was transformed deeply within and also received a physical healing in her body.

Aside from the brief lull I will mention later in the book, I have never stopped speaking in tongues. We worship the Lord in tongues daily and intercede in tongues for ourselves and for others. Being baptized in the Holy Spirit has given us a deep love for the Lord Jesus Christ, a love for the Bible and for prayer, and a greater love and compassion for others. It has brought great joy and fulfillment into our lives, and a ministry that has taken us to over forty nations of the world.

From Cowardice to "Holy Boldness"

And when she saw Peter warming himself, she looked upon him, and said, And thou also wast with Jesus of Nazareth. But he denied ... .

The Baptism in the Holy Spirit and Inner Healing

And he denied it again. ... He began to curse and to swear, saying, I know not this man of whom ye speak.
Mark 14:67-68 and 70-71

The baptism of the Holy Spirit delivers us from fear and makes us bold.

Peter denied Jesus three times and even cursed during the third denial. On the Day of Pentecost, this same Peter was baptized in the Holy Spirit and fire, and the Lord delivered him from a spirit of fear and from profanity. That day his fears were replaced by a courage that enabled him in the future to preach the Gospel all over the known world in the face of imprisonment and death. His life was totally changed that day.

When Jesus was arrested, Peter was not the only one who denied Him: *"Then all the disciples forsook him, and fled"* (Matthew 26:56; see also Mark 14:50). On the Day of Pentecost, these other disciples were also baptized in the Holy Spirit and fire and delivered from their fears. Their lives were dramatically changed, and they too became willing to suffer and die for the Lord.

Paul's life was cleansed, sanctified and empowered through the baptism of the Holy Spirit and speaking in other tongues. He declared, *"I thank my God, I speak with tongues more than ye all"* (1 Corinthians 14:18), and the result was a total turnaround in his life. His hatred of Christians was transformed into a burning love for Christ and His people. His driving energy to persecute and destroy Christians changed into a zeal to win souls for Christ. He was able to declare:

Laugh and Cry Your Way to Freedom

I count all things but loss for the excellency of the knowledge of Christ Jesus my Lord: for whom I have suffered the loss of all things, and do count them but dung, that I may win Christ. Philippians 3:8

In the time of the early Church virtually everyone, including the authors of the New Testament books, all the apostles and even Mary the mother of Jesus had this experience of being baptized in the Holy Spirit and speaking in other tongues. Through the baptism in the Holy Spirit, the Lord did a deep work of inner transformation and sanctification (inner healing) in Peter, in Paul, and in the lives of the other disciples. They all became *"obedient unto death"* and were transformed into firebrands for their faith. Their heart's desire became winning souls for Christ.

Different Dimensions of Being Baptized in the Holy Spirit

There are different dimensions of being baptized in the Holy Spirit, and most of us are receiving experiences far below the level God has for us. We should not be satisfied with a "light" infilling of the Holy Spirit. I speak from experience, for I received a light infilling myself. I wanted a deeper experience, so I went on a ten-day fast, and on the third day of the fast I received a life-changing refilling of the Spirit which included deliverance from an occultic evil spirit.

According to the Bible pattern, the baptism in the Holy Spirit is accompanied by a dramatic transformation in one's life, with the purifying, transforming fire of the Holy Spirit attending it. John the Baptist declared:

The Baptism in the Holy Spirit and Inner Healing

I indeed baptize you with water; but one mightier than I cometh, the latchet of whose shoes I am not worthy to unloose: he shall baptize you with the Holy Ghost and with fire. Luke 3:16

The "fire" of the Holy Spirit produces much cleansing and inner healing in those who experience it.

One elderly Australian minister told me, "I laughed off and on for three days after being baptized in the Holy Spirit. I was forever changed." Another minister said, "After being filled with the Holy Spirit, I wept for three days. My life was transformed." Both of these men became prayer warriors and mighty men of God.

The baptism in the Holy Spirit often brings with it weeping and holy laughter. Both are forms of self-travail. This travail from the innermost part of one's being can include contractions of the stomach muscles, *"groanings"* (see Romans 8:26) and even screaming (see the following chapter). Anointed screaming, a loud crying from deep within, releases the emotional poisons of bitterness and other hurts in our lives. It is often an important part of life-changing self-travail. Deep laughter in the Spirit is also a form of self-travail that can lead to deep inner healing. Also, such laughter frequently triggers deep sobbing or crying. These manifestations of the Spirit are powerful in releasing us from the hurts of the past and in inner cleansing.

Drunk in the Spirit for Three Days

A lovely saint of God received the baptism in the Holy Spirit in about 1910. For three days she could only speak in tongues. She could not speak a word in English. The Lord did a deep work of inner transformation in her life. She became deep in prayer, faith and inner holiness, and from her family line came a number of outstanding men and women of God, one of whom ministered in over eighty nations of the world, and another who ministered in over a hundred and fifty nations of the world.

Deeply Baptized in the Holy Spirit

As you hunger for more of God, you can be refilled with the Holy Spirit and receive a greater anointing in your life too. Jesus promised:

> *Blessed are they which do hunger and thirst after righteousness: for they shall be filled.* Matthew 5:6

> *Blessed are ye that hunger now: for ye shall be filled.*
> Luke 6:21

How can your hunger for the Lord grow? The first step is to ask God to increase your hunger for Him. He will do it. He has promised:

> *For it is God who works in you both to will and to do for His good pleasure.* Philippians 2:13, NKJ

Then take these further steps to increase your hunger for Him. Make more time for Him. Set priorities for the things of the Spirit. Give up some of your television time. Give up certain magazines or hobbies. Get up thirty min-

The Baptism in the Holy Spirit and Inner Healing

utes earlier in the morning. Pray at least thirty minutes a day in tongues and study the Word of God.

Each of us needs to be deeply baptized in the Holy Spirit and to have rivers of living water flowing from deep within us. Sing in tongues. Praise and worship in tongues. Intercede and do spiritual warfare in tongues. Let the *"river"* flow out through you.

Your hunger will quickly grow, and your life will be transformed, for Jesus declared:

> *He that believeth on me, as the scripture hath said, out of his belly shall flow rivers of living water. (But this spake he of the Spirit, which they that believe on him should receive: for the Holy Ghost was not yet given; because that Jesus was not yet glorified.)*
> John 7:38-39

The Key to Life-Changing Inner Healing

Whenever I minister inner healing to individuals who do not speak in tongues, with their permission I pray for them to speak fluently in tongues, usually in three or more unknown tongues. We all need to have great freedom in speaking in other tongues. This fluency, or ease, in speaking in tongues opens our spirits to the deep sanctifying work of the Holy Spirit. It becomes much easier for us to open up to self-travail, and such self-travail is normally essential to life-transforming, quick inner healing.

Because many who are baptized in the Holy Spirit have shallow experiences, those experiences are too often not accompanied by inner healing or deliverance. Most of us do far too little singing, praying and spiritual warfare in tongues. We need much more teaching in the Body of Christ on the life-changing importance of regular praying in tongues. It should be at least thirty minutes a day. We need a revelation of the awesome benefits of speaking much in tongues, including greater intimacy with God, the deepening of our prayer lives, and an increased hunger for the things of God.

Deep or Shallow?

If any of the following conditions exist in your life, your experience in the Holy Spirit probably has not been deep enough, and you need to seek God more fully:

1. You still have difficulty speaking easily or deeply in tongues, or you always whisper or speak quietly in tongues.

You are probably fearful that at times you are making the words up. Such doubt and unbelief keep it shallow. Fear not! Here is some life-changing good news: Your tongues are always from the Spirit and never from the flesh. Jesus said:

> *If a son shall ask bread of any of you that is a father, will he give him a stone? or if he ask a fish, will he for a fish give him a serpent? Or if he shall ask an egg, will he offer him a scorpion? If ye then, being evil, know how to give good gifts unto your children: how much more shall your heavenly Father give the Holy Spirit to them that ask him?* Luke 11:11-13

The Baptism in the Holy Spirit and Inner Healing

Confess this truth over and over again, that you are getting bread and not a stone, a fish and not a serpent. You will soon get the revelation that your speaking or singing in tongues is always from the Lord and you are never making it up. This truth will bring a wonderful change in your prayer life. It will free you to speak more deeply in the tongues God has already given you and to receive new ones.

2. You have never spoken in more than one or two languages in tongues.

The Word of God refers to *"divers kinds of tongues"* (1 Corinthians 12:10) or *"diversities of tongues"* (1 Corinthians 12:28), which simply means "many" and "varied." Countless thousands of Spirit-filled Christians, including Pattie and me, speak in many unknown tongues, and this blesses our lives greatly.

God has this experience for you also. By faith, start speaking in a different language, then another new one, until you have spoken in four or five new tongues. Speaking a new language in tongues will be like shifting from first to second gear. Then the next new tongue will be like shifting into third gear. By the third or fourth tongue, you will be in overdrive! Isn't that exciting?

Never stop growing and deepening your experience. Later, speak in four or five more languages. Remember that you will always get bread and not a stone, a fish and not a serpent. Your language will not be made up or copied. It will be from God. His Word promises you this. Always stand on what His Word, His truth, declares, not on your feelings about His truth.

3. **You haven't felt a strong desire to pray in tongues, to read the Bible, or to go to Spirit-led meetings.**

THESE ARE ALL SURE INDICATIONS THAT YOUR EXPERIENCE IN THE HOLY SPIRIT HAS NOT BEEN DEEP ENOUGH. When you have a deep infilling of the Holy Spirit, a much deeper desire for the things of the Spirit will come into your life as a result.

What Can You Do to Receive a Greater Infilling of the Holy Spirit?

If you are already filled with the Holy Spirit, to deepen your experience, do this:

1. **For three days, shout loudly for thirty minutes in tongues each day.**

This will help to release suppressed emotions and bring new joy, and the gifts of the Spirit will often begin to flow more freely in your life.

Is shouting scriptural? Yes, it is:

> *And it came to pass, when the people heard the sound of the trumpet, and the people SHOUTED WITH A GREAT SHOUT, that the wall fell down flat, so that the people went up into the city, every man straight before him, and they took the city.* Joshua 6:20

> *And when the ark of the covenant of the LORD came*

The Baptism in the Holy Spirit and Inner Healing

into the camp, all Israel SHOUTED WITH A GREAT SHOUT, so that the earth rang again.

1 Samuel 4:5

Also, shouting in tongues, even for a few minutes, will often cause inner healing or deliverance from evil spirits to begin. You will be amazed and excited about what the Lord will do for you through shouting in tongues. He surely takes the *"foolish things of the world to confound the wise."* Try it.

Every day, when I am driving my car, I pray fervently in tongues. I shout or groan in travail and self-travail and even laugh in the Spirit. This practice has profoundly changed my life. Try this a few times in your automobile, and see what the Lord will do for you.

2. Pray or sing in tongues for twenty to thirty minutes every day.

Your intimacy with God will become greater. Your prayers will be answered more quickly. Your anointing in the Holy Spirit will grow and grow. The more you pray in tongues, the more you will enjoy it. It excites me to be with God. Even as I am typing this, I am looking forward with anticipation to getting into my car for a long session of praying in tongues, travailing in the Spirit, and fellowshipping with my Friend, my Savior, God's Son, Jesus.

3. When you pray or sing in tongues, be aware that you are praying or singing to Jesus.

As you speak in tongues, don't make the mistake I did for years. I prayed to the air, the floor or the walls, and not to God! God corrected me and told me He was in the room with me and that I must pray to Him, not to the air. He told me to be aware of His presence and even to picture Him in front of me as I prayed. This enlarged my prayer life and my intimacy with God.

Do the same thing. BY FAITH, picture Jesus in front of you. You often will begin to see Him in vision, even with your eyes open! EVEN AT THIS MOMENT, see Him in front of you. Look at Him. Let the sobbing come.

4. By faith, change from one language in tongues to another.

You will get bread and not a stone, a fish and not a serpent. You can do it, and it will deepen your prayer life greatly. DO IT NOW!

5. Seek more inner healing.

Conclusion

Being baptized in the Holy Spirit DEEPLY not only brings more power, joy and a great love for Jesus into our lives, but it also enables us to receive inner healing more easily. With a deep infilling of the Holy Spirit, you will find it easier to *Laugh and Cry Your Way to Freedom* and be *Changed Into His Image Through Inner Healing*.

Chapter 4

Inner Healing Through Self-Travail

Therefore are my loins filled with pain: pangs have taken hold upon me, as the pangs of a woman that travaileth. Isaiah 21:3

Likewise the Spirit also helpeth OUR infirmities: for we know not what we should pray for as we ought: but the Spirit itself maketh intercession for US with groanings which cannot be uttered. Romans 8:26

Blessed are they that mourn: for they shall be comforted. Matthew 5:4

Through travailing prayer we can powerfully intercede for the unsaved, for Christians, for government leaders, or even for entire nations. Such intercession involves spiritual warfare and the birthing of miracles. Self-travail, the travailing for one's own rejection, hurts, sins or other needs, is the key to rapid, life-transforming inner healing and deliverance — the work of inner sanctification. Such travail is not a cry of self-pity, but an opening of inner wounds to let the poisons of abuse, bitterness and rejection out so that we can be set free and be healed.

Both travail and self-travail include sobbing (with or without tears), groanings, loud crying (even crying out in anointed screams at times), and deep holy laughter. It usually comes upon Christians by the Holy Spirit when He chooses. However, the Holy Spirit wants us, by faith, to cooperate with Him and allow Him to bring travail and self-travail upon us with great frequency.

The great Azusa Street revival of 1906 in Los Angeles was the beginning of the outpouring of the Pentecostal experience in America — the experience of the baptism in the Holy Spirit and speaking in other tongues. For the next fifty years or so, the inner work of sanctification was emphasized among Spirit-filled people. In church meetings and home prayer meetings, long periods were given to weeping in repentance for uncleanness, bad attitudes and other sins, both before and after being filled with the Holy Spirit. During this time of weeping, an important form of self-travail, much inner healing and cleansing took place. The result was dramatically changed lives and the manifestation of great holiness and miracle-working power. We clearly need more of this today.

Sister Edith Ward Heflin, a pioneer of faith, described to us how her husband, Wallace, Sr., would lie on the floor by his bed, crying out in loud, agonizing travail for souls. Since then, I have often heard other individuals cry out in this way when they were in deep travail for the salvation of others. I have also read of many sinners, in the revivals

Inner Healing Through Self-Travail

of George Whitefield, Charles Finney and others, crying out under the conviction of sin. Travail and self-travail is a ministry of the Holy Ghost, and it produces miracles in people's lives.

Sue: Only a Miracle From God Could Mend Her Life

Sue's mother didn't want her, and her abusive, alcoholic father was seldom home. From childhood she had been burning with resentment toward her parents. She hated men and trusted no one.

She was injured in a dreadful auto accident at the age of fifteen, and since then no one could even lightly touch her back. As a result, she was unable to participate in most sports, and had only a limited social life.

Sue attended our revival meeting in Australia. She limped forward for prayer, hoping God would heal her aching back. The Lord revealed to me, through the word of knowledge, that unforgiveness and bitterness from her painful childhood rejection and hurts were blocking her physical healing.

As Pattie and I ministered to Sue, words of knowledge came forth from the Lord, touching her heart deeply. The electrifying power of God went through her. She crumpled into a heap on the floor, God's operating table, and for about forty-five minutes, she remained there travailing (sobbing) for herself in the Spirit. Fortunately, she stayed there until God's spiritual and physical operation was finished.

When Sue got up from the floor, she was a new person.

Laugh and Cry Your Way to Freedom

A smile and the glory of God lit up her face, replacing the painful and weary look she had borne much too long. She had forgiven her mom and dad, and the resentment was now replaced by a love for them.

Not a bit of the back pain remained. The Holy Spirit had healed both her spiritual ailments and her physical ailments. She could now look forward to a new life — sports, marriage and children. Even more importantly, she had a new, intimate relationship with the Lord Jesus.

Many of us are just as crippled as Sue was. If this has been true of your life, through inner healing you too can be healed and set free to fulfill God's plans and purposes for your life.

Dorothy: Set Free to Love and Be Loved

At the age of about twenty, Dorothy was viciously raped. During the thirty years that ensued, this tragedy destroyed two marriages and damaged her relationships with her children and friends. It filled Dorothy with bitterness, rage and shame. Her life was shipwrecked.

When Dorothy cautiously approached me at the end of my morning teaching session at a Pentecostal campmeeting, she related the torment and the shame she had been carrying for years. She whispered to me, "Can you help me? I am desperate. I can't go on living like this."

I replied, "Yes, Dorothy, I can if you will do what I tell you." Then I asked her, "Do you trust the Lord to work through me?"

She quickly answered, "Yes."

I continued, "Then raise your hands, and when I touch

Inner Healing Through Self-Travail

your head, I want you to do something that may seem strange, and even unspiritual. I want you to begin laughing at the tragedy of having been raped!" In the very next chapter, we will deal with the healing power to be found in holy laughter. It is awesome. I was sure that within a few seconds holy laughter could produce a deep emotional healing within this woman.

Dorothy was a little stunned by my very unusual spiritual advice, but in childlike simplicity, she agreed to give it a try. When I touched her head, she forced herself to begin laughing at this horror in her life. Then the anointing of holy laughter came heavily upon her. After a while the laughter changed to sobs from deep within her being. The sobbing, sometimes mixed with the laughter, continued for about thirty minutes.

Before we had begun praying, Dorothy had been unable to forgive the rapist and unable to accept herself. The bitterness, unforgiveness, fears and shame within her disappeared. At last she was free from the pain and shame of that terrible experience of thirty years before. She was free to lead a normal life — to love and to be loved.

Like Dorothy, many of us need inner healing to be set free from crippling hurts within. Jesus has made provision for your healing. Self-travail is the key.

Tim: Hundreds of Prayers But No Results!

"I've had hundreds of people pray about my back over a fifteen-year period," declared Tim, "and this is the first healing I've had in all that time. My back is completely healed. I have no more pain. I am seeing fruit in many other areas of my life as well."

Like many other men, Tim had been filled with rage and suppressed emotions due to painful emotional scars inflicted by his father in his childhood. I encouraged him to cooperate with the Holy Spirit by shouting in tongues for the release of his emotions, and of the rage he felt inside. He did this and was then able to open up to holy laughter. This, in turn, triggered a deep sobbing within him.

After we ministered to Tim on several different occasions, he was able to forgive and release his inner rage toward his father and toward others. As each stage of inner healing progressed, his back improved, until it had been totally healed. A new peace and joy came into his life, and he fell in love with his wife again. In every sense of the word, Tim was a new person, all because he learned to travail before God for the emotional pain in his life.

Conclusion

In the following chapters we will see many others, like Sue, Dorothy and Tim, who were all set free from deep emotional wounds through self-travail, God's dynamic inner healing tool. After applying these simple principles they were able to become the loving, joyous persons God had created them to be — free to love and be loved — to be givers and not takers. Each of them testified to walking in a new closeness with the Lord Jesus.

You, too, can be released from your hurts and pains from the past, and can become an instrument for setting others free. You can become the person God created you to be.

Inner Healing Through Self-Travail

Jesus wants to free you to be able to give and receive love and to enjoy greatly improved relationships with family members, friends and co-workers, and with God Himself.

Try it now. *Laugh and Cry Your Way to Freedom* and be *Changed Into His Image Through Inner Healing.*

Chapter 5

Inner Healing Through Holy Laughter

A merry heart doeth good like a medicine.
                                        Proverbs 17:22

And Sarah said, God hath made me to laugh, so that all that hear will laugh with me.   Genesis 21:6

At destruction and famine thou shalt laugh.
                                        Job 5:22

In April of 1989 while South African Evangelist Rodney Howard-Browne was conducting a meeting in upstate New York, holy laughter broke out among the people attending. This manifestation of holy laughter quickly spread until great numbers of lay people, pastors, evangelists and other Christian leaders were affected.

The meetings were spiritually fruitful. Large numbers of souls were won to the Lord, and backsliders returned to the Lord in droves.

Inner Healing Through Holy Laughter

By 1995, through his ministry, holy laughter had made its way into congregations all over America and into many foreign nations as well. As he laid his hands on Christian leaders by faith, this special anointing was imparted to them, and they took it back with them to their own place of ministry. By 1997 the phenomenon had reached worldwide proportions.

Thousands of Christian leaders and multiplied thousands of Christian lay people have had their lives transformed by this unusual outpouring of the Spirit.

Why Is God Using Holy Laughter to Bring Revival?

Many people question why God would use laughter to bring revival. The most important reason is that it produces inner healing, and with the healing comes an inner holiness and a more intimate relationship with God. Holy laughter also frequently triggers, or releases, deep sobbing or crying (self-travail), which is even more powerful in releasing God's people from the hurts of the past.

All over the world, God's Spirit is leading individuals into an intimate relationship with Him. He desires a deep inner work of transformation. He is looking for those whom He can conform to the image of His Son.

Because of a special anointing upon his life, the holy laughter we are witnessing in Rodney Howard-Browne's meetings (and now in many other meetings) comes spontaneously. It is unplanned, and not by man's efforts or methods.

Laugh and Cry Your Way to Freedom

Holy Laughter by Faith

Almost every manifestation of the Spirit that comes spontaneously, however, can also come by an act of faith. Other manifestations in this same category include dancing in the Spirit and speaking in tongues. As you step out in faith and begin worshipping or praising the Lord in the dance, God's anointing will be upon it. Whenever you speak or sing in tongues by faith, God will anoint it. It will always be from God.

In the same away, as you begin to laugh in obedience to the promptings of the Spirit, what you are doing will be "in the Spirit" and not in the flesh. It will be "holy" laughter. As we have seen, you will receive *"bread"* and not *"a stone,"* *"fish"* and not *"a serpent."* The Holy Spirit won't force you to laugh. By faith, you must begin. It will be from God! The blessings from it will change your life.

Our Inner Healing Ministry to the Irish in 1976

History reveals that over a period of several hundred years the rulers of England cruelly persecuted the Irish. This caused the hearts of the Irish to become bitter and hardened. They were unable to cry or sob for their childhood hurts — the key to deep inner healing.

What could I do to help them? The Holy Spirit unfolded the answer. He revealed that if I could get the emotionally wounded Irish, in simple childlike faith, to open up to holy laughter for their hurts, their lives would be transformed.

But how could I get them to receive this manifestation

Inner Healing Through Holy Laughter

of the Holy Spirit? Didn't it come only spontaneously? The Holy Spirit taught me that such laughter could also come by faith. The Lord instructed me to:

1. Have individuals pray loudly in tongues.

2. Lay hands on their heads, and instruct them to instantly stop speaking in tongues and, by faith, to start laughing.

As I ministered to them in this manner, in the mighty name of Jesus, one person after another burst into holy laughter. I discovered, to my amazement, that after a few moments of such laughter, most individuals began to have self-travail, sobbing and crying deeply for the hurts in their lives. Often holy laughter and crying were mixed together.

It was a glorious time of God's anointing falling heavily upon the Irish people, and one life after another was transformed.

The inability of the Irish to cry or to sob had been overcome by the Holy Spirit's manifestation of holy laughter. We must all learn to open up to this blessing by faith. It's easy. It will work for you, and your life will be transformed too.

Elizabeth: Set Free by Holy Laughter

Elizabeth, a young Irish sister, was strongly advised by her doctor not to come to our meeting. She was close to a nervous breakdown and was desperate for a miracle. She came forward for prayer, and we ministered to her for her deep-seated childhood hurts. She did not cry or sob. She just laughed, and laughed and laughed. She continued laughing for an entire hour. As a result, her whole countenance changed. She was smiling and relaxed and radiated peace because of the inner healing she experienced through holy laughter.

Elizabeth was set free from her childhood hurts, from much buried rage, and from her frayed nerves — a great miracle from the Lord. To our wonderful God be the glory.

Ralph: Rejected by Father and Mother

Ralph was tall, thin and very tense. He was full of rage and childhood hurts. His early years in life had been ones of rejection by both his father and his mother. As we laid hands on Ralph for holy laughter, he instantly began laughing and crying at the same time. At times he stopped, and we prayed for him to continue laughing. This went on for an hour or more.

Later, he said he felt like a thousand volts of electricity were zapping through him as he laughed and cried in the Spirit. The laughter pulled out the "stopper" from his container of childhood bitterness and rejection, and the pain poured out like water.

> *Looking diligently lest any man fail of the grace of God; lest any root of bitterness springing up trouble you, and thereby many be defiled.* Hebrews 12:15

The root of bitterness was removed from Ralph, and he

was able to forgive his parents deeply for the first time. Tension that had built up over many years left him, and a deep peace came into his life. Our God is truly able to deliver!

How Did It Come?

You may wonder how holy laughter came so easily to Elizabeth and Ralph? Did it come spontaneously? No! It came as they willingly followed the directions of the Holy Spirit.

They first prayed loudly in tongues. Then we "laid hands on them" and told them to stop tongues and, by faith, to begin to laugh. They were obedient, and holy laughter flowed forth.

It is just that simple! It works because it is not man's method but that of the Holy Spirit.

Holy Laughter and Its Impact on Our Ministry

Holy laughter has become a major Holy Spirit "tool" or method we use to set thousands of people free from deep rejection, anger, self-hatred and hurts of the past. Holy laughter is also a tool of spiritual warfare. I laugh at my trials, at my disappointments, and even at Satan, for it brings me a deep certainty in my soul that Christ has made me "more than a conqueror" over all the things that would try to hinder me. This has opened me up to new dimensions in prayer, enabling me to receive deep inner healing and deliverance that I had never been able to receive before. I can now open up much more deeply to crying, groaning and sobbing before the Lord. Holy laughter can do the same for you.

The Bible says, *"A merry heart doeth good like medicine"* (Proverbs 17:22). Our Bible is full of scriptures on joy, on rejoicing, on praising, on clapping our hands, and even on dancing, for there are great blessings that come into our lives through joy. Joy is medicine to our bodies, to our emotions, to our minds, and to our relationships. As the Word of God teaches:

> *For the kingdom of God is not meat and drink; but righteousness, and peace, and joy in the Holy Ghost.*
> Romans 14:17

> *The joy of the Lord is your strength.*
> Nehemiah 8:10

Holy laughter is a great key to moving into the peace and joy of the Lord, and that joy produces energy and health in us.

Laughing at Trials

The most important time to laugh (or praise God) is when you don't want to, when circumstances are screaming at you to be negative. Your cash flow is low. Your bills are overdue. You have lost your job. Your spouse has just left you for someone else. At such times, you must laugh at the circumstances and praise God for the victory.

Inner Healing Through Holy Laughter

But my God shall supply all your need according to his riches in glory by Christ Jesus.
                                        Philippians 4:19

Laughter is a language of faith, a language of victory, and a language of joy.

God Commands Laughter

One day Job seemed to be having a very bad day. The Sabeans stole all his oxen and asses and slew all the servants who guarded them except one. Then lightning came from Heaven and burned up his sheep. After that, the Chaldeans stole his camels. A windstorm came upon the house where all his children were gathered for a party and they were all killed. Not long afterward, Satan struck Job with painful boils all over his body.

Job had lost his children, his health and his wealth. So what advice did the Lord give him? He didn't tell Job to pray, to fast, or even to trust Him, but He did give Job a key to victory that is valid for all of us. The Holy Spirit said to Job through one of his friends:

At destruction and famine thou shalt laugh.
                                        Job 5:22

God was saying to Job (and to us) that we must laugh in faith at the tragedies in our lives. We must get rid of our self-pity and anger, and trust Him to bring us into victory.

God knew that the quickest way for Job to move out of

self-pity and depression into faith would be to begin laughing at his trials. Likewise, when you will be obedient to laugh when you don't want to, God will perform miracles for you. Your laughing will quickly bring joy and victory into your life.

Pattie and I Laughed Over Our Destroyed Vehicle

Several years ago a Christian friend repaired about twenty-five problem areas on our lovely, white, four-door Toyota. This included work on the transmission, a tune-up, extensive brake work, rust spots removed, cassette recorder repaired and even our broken radio antenna replaced. We were getting our vehicle into shape for a journey from Los Angeles, California, to Richmond, Virginia

Not long after everything was fixed, I drove over to Glendale one day to do some shopping. I took the Central-Brand exit into Glendale and waited patiently for the red light at Brand to change to green. I began a left turn onto Brand. Then it seemed that lightning struck. A young businessman sped through the red light and smashed into our car. It was a total loss.

Because the car was an older model, the insurance settlement we received was less than half of what it would cost to replace the vehicle. In spite of much resistance inside of me, with Pattie's encouragement, I laughed and laughed at the accident and praised God for the trial.

I certainly wasn't happy that the car was destroyed. I was laughing because I believed God would bring good out of the accident. I kept laughing and praising God until I felt a release of victory. I believed God would give us a better car!

All Things Work Together for Good

I have experienced over and over in my life that the promise of God is true:

> *And we know that all things work together for good to them that love God, to them who are the called according to his purpose.* Romans 8:28

In His perfect timing, following that trial of our faith, God guided us and we were able to replace our Toyota with a much newer and finer car, a Pontiac Bonneville SSE. It had a near-perfect beige leather interior and a brilliant, gold-colored exterior. It looked like a new car — inside and out. What a great miracle! We were so grateful to God for His provision.

Holy laughter works. It gets rid of fear and unbelief and produces faith.

When we submit to God, even in the trials of life, all things do work together for our good, and one way of proving our submission to Him is through exhibiting an attitude of praise and laughter.

God is continuing to bring miracle after miracle into my life — as I continue, in faith, to laugh and praise Him for my trials, and to thank Him for my miracles before I see them. When we *"walk by faith, not by sight,"* He is pleased.

Let us laugh our way through every trial, and learn to live in the provision, peace and joy of the Lord.

Laugh and Cry Your Way to Freedom

David: A New Heart Through Holy Laughter

David, a large black brother, had a spiritual "burden" for the street people, and he had won many of them to the Lord. In three days, he was scheduled to undergo a dangerous heart operation. He had been warned, however, by his doctors that there was a real possibility that he might die on the operating table. This would produce great fear within anyone.

This type of fear makes it difficult for a person to have faith for healing. I sensed that the Lord wanted to delivered David from his fear through holy laughter. "Brother," I said to him, "I want to pray for you. God wants to heal you. I am going to speak an unusual word. Will you laugh when I say that word?"

He replied, "Yes, I will."

"I am going to pray for you now," I said, "but when I say the word 'operation' I want you to laugh."

He agreed.

I asked him to pray loudly in tongues for a while, then I laid hands on his head and spoke the word "Operation." David immediately began to laugh, and he laughed and laughed in the Spirit about the greatly feared operation. I repeated that word operation several times, and he kept laughing at it. Then I told him that I wanted him to laugh at the word "death," and he did this two or three times. David kept laughing for about fifteen or twenty minutes — until all fear of the upcoming operation and of the possibility of death was gone.

I didn't even have to pray for David's heart. During the laughter, the power of God flowed into his body and gave him a new one. When he went back to the doctor several days later, more x-rays were taken, and what they saw amazed them. "You have the heart of a young person," his doctor told him. The operation was canceled. God used the manifestation of holy laughter to accomplish this creative miracle. God has a miracle for you through holy laughter.

Michael: Pained From His Parents' Divorce

Twelve-year-old, curly-headed Michael was in deep emotional pain from parental rejection and the pains of his parents' divorce. When I laid hands on him and directed him to "laugh," he fully cooperated with the Holy Spirit and began laughing deeply in the Spirit at the tragedies in his life. His mother later wrote about what happened. *"My son, Michael, had a mighty touch from the Lord. For two hours straight he laughed and cried his way to freedom from the terrible hurts he received when his father left home, and then again he had another good dose of Holy Ghost laughter the last night, being set free of the pains I had caused and the hatred of his brother through jealousy. ... He's a different boy. ... We are close now. He is no longer a rejected boy who can't socialize. His grades are also improving. He now speaks with love of his father and can remember the good times. There is a compassion in him that is far beyond his years. ... God set me free also. I went forward and cried and screamed my way free. ... Praise God."*

"Priming the Pump" for the Waters of Holy Laughter to Flow

Can you laugh when you don't feel like laughing? Can

you force laughter to come, and will it be in the Spirit? Absolutely! How do you do this? How can you begin laughing in the Spirit? The answer is "by priming the pump." I'm a city person, but my father was from the country. They had hand pumps in those days and they kept a small tin cup beside the pump to prime it. A small amount of water had to be poured into the pump to give it suction, then the handle was worked up and down a few times, and soon water was gushing out in a great stream.

There is a "priming of the pump" that applies in many spiritual areas. Most of us have probably done this even if we didn't know about this spiritual principle. We have all learned to praise the Lord when we didn't feel like it or want to do it. As we compelled ourselves to praise God, the anointing came upon us, the presence of God increased, and we began to feel better and better. We were priming the pump.

We can do the same thing by jumping or leaping in the Spirit. The Bible says:

> *Blessed are ye, when men shall hate you ... and cast out your name as evil, for the Son of man's sake.* *REJOICE YE IN THAT DAY, AND LEAP FOR JOY.* Luke 6:22-23

When we are persecuted, disappointed, hurt or rejected, we must often force ourselves to praise the Lord. We trust Him to know what is best for us, and we make a decision to praise Him, even when our flesh is fighting it. That is what we mean by "priming the pump." It works because God always anoints what he commands us to do.

Begin to force yourself to laugh at the pains of life — a laughter of faith. This will release you from anger, hurts, fears and self-pity and bring you into a place of joy and faith.

"Hee, Hee, Ha, Ha, Ho, Ho!"

About seven years ago, nearly twenty years after the revelations on holy laughter in Ireland, God revealed to me an awesomely important way to prime the pump. As I reveal this simple, yet life-changing, truth to you, keep in mind what the Bible says about God choosing the foolish things of the world:

> *But God hath chosen the foolish things of the world to confound the wise; and God hath chosen the weak things of the world to confound the things which are mighty.*   1 Corinthians 1:27

The Lord revealed that I should have individuals focus on their emotional pain, pray loudly in tongues, and then say, "Hee, hee, ha, ha, ho, ho" several times. As they were obedient to the Lord and did this, holy laughter was triggered. Deep inner healing was experienced, and lives were profoundly changed.

The Lord Himself called it the "Hee-hee, ha-ha, ho-ho! revelation." I now use this Holy Spirit method extensively, and many lives are blessed by it. When used as the Holy Spirit directs, it produces amazing results.

Laugh and Cry Your Way to Freedom

You Can Do It

When you are feeling discouraged or have hurts that need healing, close your eyes, force yourself to raise your head, and begin praising the Lord in tongues or English for a minute or two. Then begin saying "Hee, hee, ha, ha, ho, ho!" and repeat it several times. If you cooperate with the Holy Spirit, this will usually release a flow of holy laughter.

If that doesn't work, try saying, "Ho, ha, hee, hee" or "ho, ho, hee, hee, ha, ha!" This is not being silly. It is being spiritual! God takes the *"foolish things of the world to confound the wise."* These words are holy words, heavily anointed by the Holy Spirit, and amazingly effective. To the natural mind, this "method" is so absurd, so ridiculous, but it will usually produce holy laughter in anyone. God's methods bear fruit.

If your spouse has just hurt you deeply, your child has just wrecked the automobile, and the insurance expired three days ago, raise your head and say, "Ha, ha, husband (or wife); ho, ho, automobile; hee, hee, expired insurance." Soon the laughter will come. Try it. It works. Fear and unbelief will depart, and faith and joy will come. Be childlike. Be humble. Laugh your way to victory!

As you begin to laugh, force yourself to continue, and not to go back into English or tongues. Laugh, even if you think you are making it up. You are getting *"bread"* and not *"a stone,"* *"a fish"* and not *"a serpent"* (Luke 11:11-13). You will be priming the pump, and soon you will feel the laughter coming spontaneously.

Inner Healing Through Holy Laughter

Praising God for Trials

Praise God for trials. Laugh at them, count them all joy and leap for joy because of them. When you do this, you are putting God in control of your life. Otherwise, people and circumstances will control your life and your emotions. As a result, you will live with a "victim" mentality instead of a "more than a conqueror" mentality.

Don't blame your past for your problems, and don't condemn yourself. You are not a victim unless you choose to be one. Regardless of your childhood, education or other negative circumstances, God has a plan of victory for you. He will even bring good out of the tragedies in your life. Start laughing at them.

Even God Laughs

He that sitteth in the heavens shall laugh: the Lord shall have them in derision. Psalm 2:4

The Lord shall laugh at him: for he seeth that his day is coming. Psalm 37:13

God laughs at principalities and powers, and He laughs at Satan himself. God knows that the victory is His, and He knows that we also have the victory for it has been purchased for us through the shed blood of Jesus Christ. Paul wrote:

Now thanks be unto God, which always causeth us to triumph in Christ. 2 Corinthians 2:14

Laugh and Cry Your Way to Freedom

Bill: Full of Rage

Bill had pastored a number of churches. He preached hard and legalistically and continually wounded his sheep, so he lost one church after another.

From a dysfunctional, abusive childhood, he was wounded on the inside and was full of rage. He had received little love in his childhood and didn't know how to give love. Because of this, his relationships with his wife, children and friends had been badly damaged. He was already out of the ministry, and his personal life was falling apart.

Despite the fact that he had sought help for years and had been prayed for many times to be freed from his emotional pain and rage, he was still bound. In desperation, he decided to make a long trip to see us.

Bill had built many walls around his heart. This insulated him from change, from "losing control" of his life. However, he knew his life was headed for further disaster unless he changed. He desperately needed much inner healing.

I sensed that the deep work the Lord wanted to perform in Bill would have to take place when he was praying alone. I instructed him about his need for deep self-travail, the deep "groanings" of Romans 8:26. His rage and his buried screams needed to be released by the Holy Spirit. In addition, his deep wounds from his abusive childhood needed to be healed.

"Get alone," I told him, "where no one can hear you, and bring your torment, your rage, your hurts to the Lord. Pray loudly in tongues, shout in tongues, and then, by faith, say 'Hee, hee, ha, ha, ho, ho!' and let the laughter and the screams come."

"Bill," I continued, "you may be amazed at the rage, the anger and the screams that come forth from you when you do this, but don't be afraid. God is setting you free."

With some skepticism, Bill followed my instructions, and this is what he later related to me. "Brother Chappell, I did what you told me. To be honest, I thought it was total foolishness, and yet I had nothing to lose. As soon as I began to say 'Hee, hee, ha, ha, ho, ho!' a spiritual explosion took place. I sobbed and screamed and screamed some more. Soon I began laughing at the pains of the past, and then more screams came. This went on for about two hours. My whole life has been changed — my marriage, my finances, my personality, my relationship with my children, and my closeness to God."

With sincerity and childlike trust, do what Bill did, and see what God will do for you.

Holy Laughter Releases Forgiveness Toward Others

Laughter will release forgiveness, rid you of bitterness, and bring inner healing into your life like it did for Bill and Bob. Holy laughter will help release deep forgiveness in your life so you can be free from the emotional pain of hurts and be free to live at a new level of love, joy and peace.

Pride — a fear of looking foolish in front of people and a fear of losing control — can easily hold you back from laughing. Religious tradition can cause you to believe laughter isn't necessary or even scriptural. But it will be worth it all if you just give it a try. You will know forgiveness is complete when the emotional pain is gone from the hurt or disappointment, and a deep peace is present. Holy laughter, sobbing and tears are all powerful in releasing unforgiveness and bitterness. Cooperate fully with the Holy Spirit and let Him do this for you.

As you learn more about inner healing for your own life, God will bring hurting people to you for ministry. Likewise, you can minister to them for laughter for the hurts in their lives, and God will bring mighty releases within them too.

"Except Ye Become as Little Children"

As we have seen, God uses *"the foolish things of this world."* Jesus also taught us to become *"as little children":*

> *Verily I say unto you, Except ye be converted, and become as little children, ye shall not enter into the kingdom of heaven.* Matthew 18:3

To enter the greatness of God's blessings, you must come to Him with a childlike simplicity, hunger and trust, putting down your pride and saying, "Here I am, Lord. Do whatever it takes to set me free. If I have to laugh, if I have to scream, if I have to dance or jump, Lord, I will do it. I must get set free. I want all You have for my life. Here I am, Lord. Do what needs to be done. I'm willing to look foolish. I'm determined to be set free." When you come with that attitude, you will be set free. You will be blessed greatly. The glory of God will fill your life in a mighty way.

I am hungry to be continually changed. I am hungry to be closer to God, to know Him better, and to be a greater blessing to my family and to the family of God. I believe that's what you want too, and that's the reason you are reading this book.

Conclusion

Holy laughter has been a great blessing in my life and in the lives of thousands of others, in enabling the Holy Spirit to change us on the inside, to bring new dimensions of sanctification within through inner healing and deliverance. Through holy laughter, the Lord will do the same for you and, through you, for many others. So start laughing. *Laugh and Cry Your Way to Freedom* and be *Changed Into His Image Through Inner Healing.*

Chapter 6

Inner Healing Through Forgiveness of Others, Oneself and God

And grieve not the holy Spirit of God ... . Let all bitterness, and wrath, and anger, and clamour, and evil speaking, be put away from you, with all malice: And be ye kind one to another, tenderhearted, forgiving one another, even as God for Christ's sake hath forgiven you.   Ephesians 4:30-32

Judge not, and ye shall not be judged: condemn not, and ye shall not be condemned: forgive, and ye shall be forgiven.   Luke 6:37

The Holy Spirit is grieved by our grumbling, our complaining, our lack of kindness, our lack of deeply forgiving others from the heart, and we are sowing negative seeds by judging, condemning and not being willing to forgive. The reason the Holy Spirit is grieved is because He loves each of us so intensely, and He knows the great harm that

Inner Healing Through Forgiveness ...

will come into our lives and the lives of our loved ones from negative seeds of unforgiveness. Judging, condemning, complaining and unforgiveness are all intertwined. They are related to each other. They all indicate a lack of forgiveness.

What harm can come from such negative sowing of unforgiveness? Damaged health, broken marriages, ruined relationships with children, with other Christians, and with fellow employees are just some of the harmful effects that come to the unforgiving. Since forgiveness and the release of bitterness which it engenders are so important, we must learn what true forgiveness is, what it isn't and how we can effectively forgive.

What Forgiveness Is Not

1. Forgiveness is not weakness, but strength.
2. Forgiveness does not restore trust, but opens the door to the possibility of reestablishing such trust. Forgiveness is a free gift. Trust must be earned.
3. Forgiveness often does not include a restoration of a relationship, friendship or marriage. You must forgive your divorced or separated spouse, ex-prayer partner, ex-boss or ex-pastor, but the relationship often will not be restored.
4. Forgiveness is not condoning sin or saying that what was done is okay. If a person has sinned against you and/or God, he or she is guilty and must answer to God. He has said:

Dearly beloved, avenge not yourselves, but rather give

> *place unto wrath: for it is written, Vengeance is mine;*
> *I will repay, saith the Lord.* Romans 12:19

Then, What Is Forgiveness?

Forgiveness is releasing a person from a debt owed to us. We give up our right to get revenge for the wrong someone has done to us. We lose our desire to "get even."

In the Old Testament, some revenge was permitted, but only as mercy to avoid greater retribution. God allowed *"an eye for an eye, and a tooth for tooth,"* but no more. He did not allow two eyes for one eye, or two teeth for one tooth.

In the New Testament, the dispensation of grace, we are commanded to turn the other cheek, go the extra mile and bless our enemies. Jesus instructed us:

> *But I say unto you, Love your enemies, bless them that curse you, do good to them that hate you, and pray for them which despitefully use you, and persecute you.* Matthew 5:44

If we can develop a lifestyle of praying blessings for those who hurt, disappoint and reject us, instead of criticizing and complaining, our lives will be dramatically blessed. We will live in new joy, peace and love.

Have We Forgiven?

Have we really forgiven our parents for our childhood hurts? Have we forgiven our enemies, friends and loved ones who have hurt us so deeply? Many of us may have

Inner Healing Through Forgiveness ...

forgiven in our minds, but only partially from our hearts. The poison of bitterness toward others must be drained from our inner man through inner healing. Then the forgiveness will be complete. Otherwise, the negative reaping from unforgiveness and bitterness will defile our lives and the lives of those we most love. Every relationship in our lives will be negatively affected. The very ones we most want to love and bless we will hurt the most.

Malcolm: A Financial Curse

Malcolm's rent was unpaid, his car payment was due, his cupboards were bare, and his gas tank was nearly empty. An expert in computer technology — young, energetic, always well-liked and respected — Malcolm, for no apparent reason, had not only recently lost his job, but could not get another. Although he was highly qualified in his field of work, one job interview after another fell through. In his first interview, his job application got lost. After his second interview, a much less qualified individual was employed. The third job opportunity suddenly disappeared for no apparent reason. With the fourth job opportunity, the employer tried to locate him, and when he could not, he gave the job to someone else.

Why was all this happening? A few weeks before, Malcolm had received the greatest emotional shock of his life. He discovered that his attractive, brunette wife Sally had been committing adultery with one of his best friends, a good-looking and young business executive. A few days later, she left Malcolm and moved in with the other man.

When this happened, Malcolm's world caved in, and

he became furious at his wife and at his former friend. Bitterness, like a cancerous growth, became deeply imbedded within him and began to eat away at his emotional and spiritual life. An evil spirit gleefully looked at this open door, provided by the sin of unforgiveness, and brought a financial curse into Malcolm's life. Within a few weeks his boss had fired him, and his life was in a downward spiral.

Malcolm had sown bitterness, and now he was reaping a financial and emotional disaster. A curse entered his life through the defilement of bitterness. Like many of us, he had *"let the sun go down on [his] wrath."* God warned us against it:

> *Be ye angry, and sin not: let not the sun go down upon your wrath.* Ephesians 4:26

Malcolm may have had good reason to be furious at his wife and friend, but we can never forget the fact that we live in a spiritual world which is run by strict laws, just as our natural world is. One of those unchangeable laws is the law of sowing and reaping. The Bible clearly teaches:

> *Looking diligently lest any man fail of the grace of God; lest any root of bitterness springing up trouble you, and thereby many be defiled.* Hebrews 12:15

Malcolm had become defiled by his bitterness, and this brought trouble to his life. Before very long, his finances were a disaster. He had no job, and unpaid bills were piling up. When God revealed to me how Satan had brought a financial curse into Malcolm's life, I shared this with him.

Inner Healing Through Forgiveness ...

I explained that forgiveness does not mean we condone sin, and is not a sign of weakness. I continued, "Malcolm, forgiveness is giving up the right for revenge and your fleshly desire for your wife and friend to suffer for what they have done. It involves repenting for a condemning, hateful spirit toward them and releasing them to God."

Malcolm had no right to take vengeance into his own hands. The Bible declares:

> *Dearly beloved, avenge not yourselves, but rather give place unto wrath: for it is written, Vengeance is mine; I will repay, saith the Lord.* Romans 12:19

Seeing the curse that bitterness had brought into his life, Malcolm agreed to forgive his wife and his ex-friend for their terrible disloyalty. I led him in a prayer of repentance for the sin of condemnation and bitterness toward his wife and friend. He forgave them and released all bitterness to the Lord. We also prayed a long prayer of blessing over their lives to deeply establish his forgiveness of them, for Jesus commands us:

> *Love your enemies ... and pray for them which despitefully use you, and persecute you.*
> Matthew 5:44

After he had prayed this prayer, we used the name of the Lord Jesus to break the curse of poverty. Within a few days a wonderful miracle took place. He received a new job, even better than his previous one. Because of forgiveness, the bitterness was gone, the curse of poverty was broken, and his relationship with the Lord was restored.

To some degree we are all like Malcolm. We must repent of unforgiveness and bitterness toward others, toward God, and even toward ourselves. Then we need to walk in a spirit of forgiveness so that we can flow in the fullness of God's plan of emotional, spiritual and financial prosperity for us.

Harry: Full of Unforgiveness

Harry was to be operated on in three days for the chronic pain in his back. He had been told that the operation might not help, but he seemed to have no other choice. He simply could not go on living with such awful pain. Through the word of knowledge, I understood that his back was not being healed because of buried rage and unforgiveness. Harry needed to forgive his father and mother for much rejection. He held unforgiveness toward many people, particularly women.

Harry wanted to be free from this bitterness, and he wanted to be able to forgive, but for such forgiveness to take place usually inner healing is necessary.

I had Harry shout in tongues for a minute or two, then I prayed for him to laugh loudly in the Spirit. Immediately he began to laugh, and this released loud crying and screaming, and then more laughter. For about an hour he laughed, groaned and even screamed in emotional pain as the Holy Spirit released deep-seated emotions of rage within him.

A deep spiritual operation took place in Harry that day

Inner Healing Through Forgiveness ...

involving inner healing and deliverance. His bitterness and unforgiveness disappeared. Peace and joy filled his being. He was a changed person. Soon he also became aware that all pain had left his back. He was totally healed by the power of forgiveness. He canceled the back operation and repeatedly testified of the miracle Jesus had given him.

Unforgiveness Is Often the Root Cause of Illness

Unforgiveness and the bitterness that goes with it not only block one's prayer for physical healing but in many cases actually cause physical ailments. Most arthritis and cancer are caused by buried resentments. Only recently a sister from Ohio related to me the case of her beloved father. He was an ordained minister and evangelist, but he had been severely hurt by many Christians over a period of many years and had become bitter as a result. He thought his anger was righteous indignation and that it was justified, so he had apparently never learned how important it was to forgive, regardless of the wrong done to us. "Dad died of cancer caused by bitterness," the woman told me, and I was sure she was right.

Walking in forgiveness, practicing forgiveness as a way of life, and praying blessings on those who hurt you are keys to good physical, emotional and mental health.

Sarah: Paralysis Healed by Forgiveness

A dentist had accidentally cut a nerve in Sarah's lower jaw, resulting in partial paralysis of her face. She came to

Pattie and me for a healing prayer. "Are you willing to forgive the dentist," we asked.

She replied, "I know I must. Please help me to do it."

We led her in a prayer of forgiveness for the trauma of her facial paralysis. She prayed a prayer of blessing for the dentist. We didn't even need to pray for the healing of her jaw. The paralysis left during the prayer of forgiveness and inner healing, and her jaw was totally healed. Forgiveness is powerful. It sets us free in many different areas of our lives.

Maggie: An Ulcer Caused by Bitterness and Healed by Forgiveness

In our meetings in Australia a number of years ago, Maggie, age twenty-one, came forward desiring healing for a painful stomach ulcer. By a word of knowledge I spoke these words to her: "You were hurt deeply when you were thirteen, and you need to forgive the person who hurt you."

Maggie began to cry, confessing the rage that had been in her since her early teen years. She repented and, with many tears, forgave the offender. Again, we didn't need a healing prayer. As she forgave and allowed the Holy Spirit to remove the rage within and to heal her hurting heart, she was instantly healed. All the pain from the ulcer left.

The Kingdom of God is based on sowing and reaping. The Bible says:

Be not deceived; God is not mocked: for whatsoever a

Inner Healing Through Forgiveness ...

man soweth, that shall he also reap. For he that soweth to his flesh shall of the flesh reap corruption.
Galatians 6:7

When we sow unforgiveness and the bitterness that comes from it, as Malcolm, Harry, Sarah and Maggie did, we will surely reap the curses that come from unforgiveness. When we sow good things, then we will reap blessings. When we deeply forgive, as Malcolm, Harry, Sarah and Maggie eventually did, blessings will flood into our lives. Miracles will take place. Relationships with others and with God will dramatically improve. What are we waiting for? Let us become forgiving, loving Christians.

The Many Reasons We Need to Forgive

1. Unforgiveness carries with it a root of bitterness, which will spring up and defile or contaminate our marriage partner, our children, our friends and all others we come in contact with. It will damage all of our relationships, including our relationship with God. Bitterness opens the door for Satan to bring a multitude of disasters into our lives. We must forgive and remain free from bitterness.

2. God will forgive us of our sins only when we forgive others. Jesus said:

Judge not, and ye shall not be judged: condemn not, and ye shall not be condemned: forgive, and ye shall be forgiven.
Luke 6:37

3. Unforgiving people are hurting people, and they hurt others. Forgive deeply, and allow the Holy Spirit to bring healing to your hurting heart, and this act will free you from hurting others.

4. Unforgiveness weakens our prayer power, particularly for the person for whom we are praying. The Word of God tells us:

And when ye stand praying, forgive, if ye have ought against any: that your Father also which is in heaven may forgive you your trespasses. Mark 11:25

5. Unforgiveness can cause us to become sick. It can also keep us from being healed and prevent us from keeping our healing.

6. Unforgiveness can cause or contribute to emotional (or mental) sickness.

7. Unforgiveness can cause financial curses.

8. When we fail to forgive, we will become like the person we criticize, judge or hold bitterness toward.

9. If we men fail to honor our wives (which includes forgiveness), our prayers will be hindered:

Likewise, ye husbands, dwell with them according to knowledge, giving honor unto the wife, as unto the

Inner Healing Through Forgiveness ...

weaker vessel, and as being heirs together of the grace of life; that your prayers be not hindered.
1 Peter 3:7

10. Forgiveness of the one who has hurt us is an important key to our being released from negative soul ties (bondage) with them. It is also a key to the breaking of generational curses, particularly the deep forgiveness of a mother or father.

11. We will never rise to greatness in God — greatness in ministry and greatness in relationships — until we forgive from our hearts those who have hurt us.

Hurts and Bitterness Toward Parents

As we have seen, no matter how good we think our childhood was, we have vastly more hurts and rejections than we can imagine, and most of them often remain forgotten or buried. These hurts can cause us to distrust our marriage partner in various ways (as we see our parents' negative qualities in them). Our deep forgiveness of our parents sets us free to *"cleave"* to our mate, to truly know them, to trust them, and to love them more deeply. Jesus stated:

For this cause shall a man leave father and mother, and shall cleave to his wife: and they twain shall be one flesh. Matthew 19:5

Laugh and Cry Your Way to Freedom

Deep forgiveness of our mother and father frees us to *"leave"* our parents, to become free from negative dependence on them, and to *"cleave"* in perfect godly unity to our mate.

Dinah: A Marriage in Trouble

Dinah had repeated arguments and fights with her husband. She had hidden rage toward men. The marriage was about to break up when, in desperation, she came to us for help. As Pattie and I ministered to her for inner healing, the Lord revealed to us that the root cause of her marital problem was bitterness toward her father.

When I laid hands on her and prayed for the healing of the wounds from her father's rejection, she was "slain" under the power of God, and for about thirty minutes, she sobbed deeply in self-travail. Through this travail, she was able to deeply forgive her father. This forgiveness of her father released the rage within her toward all men, including her husband, and her marriage was saved.

Patricia: "I Hate My Husband"

Several years ago, while we were ministering in Australia, Patricia approached me, also in desperation, and whispered, "I hate my husband. I want to love him, but I can't stand him. Can you help me?"

Just as with Dinah, the Holy Spirit showed me that unforgiveness toward her father was the root cause of Patricia's hatred and distrust of her husband. "The problem is your father, Patricia," I said. "Are you willing to forgive him? Are you willing to release all rage toward your father?"

She was surprised by this, but she replied, "Yes, I need help. My relationship with my father was terrible, and it's true, I do hate him."

Pattie and I began praying for her for a release from the terrible hurts and rejection from her father. She began sobbing deeply and fell out under the power of God onto the Lord's operating table.

Patricia travailed in deep sobbing for about thirty minutes. The rejection and hurts from her father were lifted from her, and her bitterness toward him was gone. She forgave her father for the terrible childhood abuse and now felt a love for him. As this hatred toward him left, her hatred toward her husband also melted away and was replaced by love. The marriage was restored.

Forgiving Our Loved Ones Can Lead to Their Salvation

Unforgiveness toward our loved ones weakens our salvation prayers for them and is a major reason why they go unsaved for years. The Bible shows we that must forgive when we stand praying:

> *For verily I say unto you, That whosoever shall say unto this mountain, Be thou removed, and be thou cast into the sea; and shall not doubt in his heart, but shall believe that those things which he saith shall come to pass; he shall have whatsoever he saith. ... Therefore I say unto you, What things soever ye de-*

sire, when ye pray, believe that ye receive them, and ye shall have them. ... And when ye stand praying, FORGIVE, IF YE HAVE OUGHT AGAINST ANY: THAT YOUR FATHER ALSO WHICH IS IN HEAVEN MAY FORGIVE YOU YOUR TRESPASSES. ... BUT IF YE DO NOT FORGIVE, NEITHER WILL YOUR FATHER WHICH IS IN HEAVEN FORGIVE YOUR TRESPASSES.

Mark 11:23-26

Jane: Her Parents Are Saved

For many years, Jane had been interceding for her parents' salvation, but they had made it clear that they wanted no part of her "religion." This rejection hurt her deeply. The Holy Spirit brought conviction that she had bitterness in her heart toward her parents because of their rejection of Christianity. After weeping for a long time on her face before God, the emotional pain of rejection was healed, and all the bitterness left. She no longer had any unforgiveness, only love, for her parents.

Within five days, both of Jane's parents were mightily saved. Jesus said that we must forgive. It is clearly unforgiveness that is hindering many of our prayers.

Mary: Her Alcoholic Husband Is Saved

For years Mary's marriage had been a living hell because of her alcoholic husband. Even after fifteen years of hard prayer from her and others, her husband seemed further from the Lord than ever.

Inner Healing Through Forgiveness ...

Then one day the Holy Spirit convicted Mary of self-righteousness, self-pity, a judgmental attitude toward her husband, and the sin of unforgiveness. She deeply repented of these sins and, with many inner-healing tears, forgave her husband for the hurts and disappointments of their marriage.

Mary's husband now had a new wife, and soon she had a new husband, for within two weeks he was delivered from alcoholism, saved and filled with the Holy Ghost. Forgiveness is powerful. Use it.

Winning Our Loved Ones

Many of us, like Jane and Mary, have been praying long and hard for an unsaved loved one. Our loved ones have some terrible habits, attitudes, selfishness or sins in their lives that really hurt, frustrate or embarrass us. When we stand praying and believing for the miracle of salvation in their lives, we must forgive them completely. Unforgiveness weakens, dilutes, our power in prayer, our power to move the mountains in our life, our power to get loved ones saved. We must deeply forgive them in order to have the power to release them from the demonic darkness that blinds them to truth and holds them back from salvation.

Conclusion

Many of us have been deeply rejected or hurt by others. Our Lord calls us to forgive as He has forgiven us. Such deep forgiveness often can only come through our being healed from the rejection and hurts of others.

Laugh and Cry Your Way to Freedom

We must allow forgiveness and blessing of others in word and deed from the heart to become a way of life. In so doing, we will sow a multitude of blessings into our own lives and into the lives of others.

You will be overjoyed at the effect this type of forgiveness will have on your relationships with others and with God. It will bring joy and peace into your life. In addition, it will be a big factor in your being healed physically and in keeping your healing. Try it. *Laugh and Cry Your Way to Freedom* and be *Changed Into His Image Through Inner Healing*.

Chapter 7

Breaking the Power of Generational Iniquity

And the LORD passed by before him, and proclaimed, The LORD, The LORD God, merciful and gracious, longsuffering, and abundant in goodness and truth, keeping mercy for thousands, forgiving iniquity and transgression and sin, and that will by no means clear the guilty; visiting the iniquity of the fathers upon the children, and upon the children's children, unto the third and to the fourth generation.

Exodus 34:6-7

One of the most important laws of the Kingdom of God is that whatever we sow we will reap (see Galatians 6:7). It is true either positively or negatively, for either bad or good. This principle works individually as well as corporately. Even whole nations reap what has been sown. The principle applies to business corporations, labor unions, church denominations, individual churches and any other group. It is true also of FAMILIES.

Laugh and Cry Your Way to Freedom

Through the sins of our "family line," we reap negatively (and positively, in generational blessings) what has been sown by previous generations. Most of our sins, demonic oppressions, lust, addictions, weaknesses, bad attitudes and failures in life have their root in this negative inheritance from our family line, which is called in the Bible, generational iniquity. While it does seem unfair that we suffer the effects of sins committed by ancestors whom we may not even know about, it is true nevertheless. The sins of our family line, going all the way back to the third and fourth generation, bring harmful occurrences and even curses into our lives.

In turn, we parents, through our sins, can bring curses upon our children and grandchildren, and these can have an evil effect unto the third and fourth generation as well. As an example, when a mother has depression, her daughter will usually have depression. If a father or a mother has a strong spirit of lust, in most cases their children will have the same problem. Dishonest parents breed dishonest children. In most cases these negative qualities go far back into the family line. For example, when dealing with a grossly immoral person, a dishonest person, a liar or an alcoholic, you will normally find parents, grandparents and great-grandparents with similar sins or weaknesses.

Victory Through the Blood of Jesus

Many of us have been incorrectly taught that once we are saved, such generational sin can no longer negatively affect our lives, that it is "under the blood." It is true that Jesus has purchased, through His precious blood, a total

Breaking the Power of Generational Iniquity

plan of salvation for us, a plan that includes forgiveness of our sins, inner sanctification, and healing of our bodies, emotions, minds and finances. It also includes deliverance from the harmful effects of generational iniquity. Christ has defeated Satan for us. Victory in every area of our lives has been provided for us through His blood poured out on the cross at Calvary. Paul wrote to the Galatians:

> *Christ hath redeemed us from the curse of the law, being made a curse for us.* Galatians 3:13

However, these blessings, although they are available to us, do not come automatically. We must learn, through the Word of God, how to receive (or appropriate) them. We must learn how to enforce the victory won at Calvary for us by Jesus through His shed blood. While we will never be free completely from our Adamic nature, God has a plan for setting us free from the negative results of generational iniquity — the root cause of many problems in our lives.

Generational Curses Resulting From Exposure to the Occult

When a family member has been involved in the occult realm, every generational sin becomes stronger, and every weakness becomes an open door for demonic oppressions. For this reason, this chapter will give great emphasis to the generational curse resulting from occultism.

The occult includes such things as astrology, ouija

boards, tarot cards, seances and Masonry. Typical of strong curses that result from dabbling in these evils are lust, abuse of children, depression, alcoholism, dishonesty, continual illness, repeated miscarriages or barrenness, being accident-prone, a family history of marriage problems, incest, fears and rebelliousness. Most of us have been far more harmed by such involvement than we realize.

The word *occult* means "hidden, mysterious or concealed." In the spiritual realm, this word encompasses all non-Christian or ungodly methods of seeking to know that which is hidden — whether dealing with the past, the present or the future. Through Satan's counterfeits, such as astrology, fortune-telling and palm reading, individuals seek to bypass God to discover hidden things. In doing so, they contact the defiling kingdom of darkness, Satan's realm, and open themselves to great tragedy.

It is often in this way that demonic spirits and curses come into people's lives and into the lives of their family members. It happened to me, and it has happened to the majority of believers, but God has total victory for all of us if we are willing to seek Him.

Occultism embraces all secret orders. Because my father was a member of the Masons, a curse came into my life, and it brought great harm to me and my family. I had to engage in spiritual warfare many times before I felt my victory was complete.

The Word of God declares:

> *The secret things belong unto the LORD our God: but those things which are revealed belong unto us and to our children for ever, that we may do all the words of this law.* Deuteronomy 29:29

Breaking the Power of Generational Iniquity

God Himself desires to reveal to us everything we need to know about the past, the present and the future, and He strictly forbids our seeking such information by Satan's methods. The Lord sternly warns us:

> *And I will cut off witchcrafts out of thine hand; and thou shalt have no more soothsayers.* Micah 5:12

> *There shall not be found among you any one that maketh his son or his daughter to pass through the fire, or that useth divination, or an observer of times, or an enchanter, or a witch, or a charmer, or a consulter with familiar spirits, or a wizard, or a necromancer. For all that do these things are an abomination unto the LORD.*
> Deuteronomy 18:10-12

God has given to the Church the indwelling Holy Spirit to reveal such dangers to us. The Lord tells us:

> *The Spirit of truth ... will guide you into all truth ... and he will shew you things to come.* John 16:13

> *My sheep hear my voice, and I know them, and they follow me.* John 10:27

The occult also includes using evil spirits, consciously or unconsciously, to supernaturally change events. This would include putting curses or blessings on people — a practice commonly known as witchcraft, or sorcery. The word *witchcraft* is often used to mean the same as "occult."

We must avoid all forms of the occult, including exposing ourselves to television programs that contain it. We must be particularly careful to screen what our children look at, including programs having to do with witches, demons, ghosts, vampires or violence. We must also be aware that rock music also carries occultic spirits.

Generational Blessings

For I the LORD thy God am a jealous God, visiting the iniquity of the fathers upon the children unto the third and fourth generation of them that hate me, and shewing mercy unto thousands of them that love me and keep my commandments.

Deuteronomy 5:9-10

It is easy to get so caught up in the importance of generational curses that we overlook generational blessings. We inherit a vast number of blessings from our family members, including intelligence, musical talent, business ability, athletic talent, a strong healthy body, mental and emotional stability, and excellent moral and spiritual qualities. The call of God often runs in family lines. We must be grateful for the family line God has placed us into, grateful for our heritage. He placed us in our particular family line for one of two reasons, and often for both reasons:

1. To be blessed by the good inheritance from it. (Most of us have been saved through the prayers of one or more "family members.")

2. For the healing of our family line. We are stew-

ards of it and need to be faithful in bringing healing to the family line.

How do we do this? We do it by breaking the power of generational curses in our line and by living a life that is sanctified and separated unto God. Thus, generational blessings will flow to our family line through our consecrated life.

My Own Generational Blessings

There were preachers on both sides of my family in generations past. My grandmother from mother's side was a Christian, and I believe her prayers and the prayers of those preachers in my family line are the reason I am a Christian today. I believe it is because of their prayers that in 1962 God laid it upon the heart of a powerful intercessor, whom we had never met, to intercede for my family. After five years of intercession by this lady, we met her daughter supernaturally and were saved and filled with the Holy Spirit through her.

We should be continually grateful for the multitude of generational blessings from the Lord, including being made in His image. Also, we should pray for those in our family line who will come after us, including our children and grandchildren.

Martha: Delivered From Inherited Spirits

Martha was desperate for ministry. She was suffering from an ulcer, arthritis and neck pains. She also was strongly oppressed by spirits of witchcraft, suicide, murder, fear of death, lust and insanity. All of these spirits were inherited from her family line. They were generational curses.

In her childhood, Martha's parents had rejected her. She had never been told she was loved, and this wounded her spirit deeply. This rejection provided an open door for evil spirits to have a strong influence in her life.

When we met Martha and saw her need, we felt a deep compassion for her. We wanted to see her set free. Through much spiritual warfare, we broke the power of the generational curse of witchcraft on her life. Then we did the same for each of the spirits that troubled her. As one by one the spirits left her, Martha laughed and sobbed in deep self-travail. God did a deep work of inner healing in her life that day, and her emotions became stable. All her fears and lust were gone.

We had not prayed specifically for her physical healing, but she was healed of ulcers, arthritis and her neck problem through the inner healing. What a great God we have! He does all things well!

Teenage Experimentation in the Occult

During the difficult, often reckless, teenage period, many get involved with various forms of the supernatural. Individuals from every age-group, INCLUDING A LARGE NUMBER OF TEENAGERS, have become involved in the occult through what is called the New Age movement. This movement involves transcendental meditation, psychic powers of various types (including ESP), astrology, seances, the use of crystals or crystal balls, Yoga, hypnosis, psychic healing (a counterfeit of divine healing), Science of the Mind, and a belief in reincarnation. Quite a few teenagers even get involved in the horrors of Satanism, and this can result in extensive spiritual, emotional and even physical abuse.

The teen years are also a time of sexual experimentation, which leads to strong negative soul ties, and transference of evil spirits, including occult spirits, from one sexual partner to the other.

There is such a great need in the Body of Christ today for a deeper understanding of how to get Christians freed from such witchcraft involvement. God may be calling you to be part of the answer to this need.

Philip: Spiritism and Asian Religions

The parents of Philip had a generational history that included much spiritism and Asian religions. Satan had a legal right to release strong demonic powers against Philip and to draw him into the occult.

Philip was a young Filipino pastor. As he sat in front of us, muscular, dignified and well-dressed, we could not help but notice the dead look on his face. He described to us his wild, rebellious teenage years. He had learned how to be violent, even to kill if need be, through kung fu, a form of karate involving strong occultic spirits. He had shut down his emotions for fear of losing control and killing someone. Because of his blocked emotions, he was unable to express the love he felt for his wife and for his congregation.

Laugh and Cry Your Way to Freedom

Philip had also experienced many hurts through rejection from both his mother and his father. Through the power of the Holy Spirit, we ministered inner healing to him for this rejection. A great deal of self-travail and holy laughter came upon him as the Lord began setting him free from the hurts of the past.

Because of his parents' family history of Asian religions and spiritism, there were strong curses in the family line. We had to do mighty spiritual warfare in the powerful name of Jesus to break these generational curses over his life.

In the name of the Lord Jesus, Philip also broke an inner vow he had made to never show his emotions. We have all made such vows that need to be broken. We will teach more on this important point in the following chapter.

Philip repented for judging his parents and for his involvement in kung fu. Through the name of Jesus and the power of the Holy Spirit, the Lord delivered him from several terrible spirits, including spirits of violence, of murder, of rage, and of lust.

Through inner healing, the Holy Spirit released Philip's true personality, and his whole facial expression changed. His lips no longer curved downward, but upward. His face was now alive. His eyes showed tenderness, peace, joy and love. He was free for the first time to be himself, and to love his wife both deeply and unselfishly. His wife's radiant joy for her "new" husband showed forth as she gazed at him with great love and tenderness. They were now more in love than ever, and his church had a "new" pastor. A year later, when we saw them again, Philip's church and his marriage were both prospering.

Breaking the Power of Generational Iniquity

We have such a great, powerful and loving God. Only through ignorance can an already defeated foe keep us in bondage. Jesus said:

> *If ye continue in my word, then are ye my disciples indeed; and ye shall know the truth, and the truth shall make you free.* John 8:31-32

God has wholeness for each of us. I want all that our Lord Jesus has for me. How about you?

Phyliss: Freed From Occultic Bondage

Phyliss, age twenty-seven, stood tall and regal at five ten. She was afraid of men, though, so she had never married. She also had great difficulty in expressing her emotions.

Phyliss had experimented with transcendental meditation, and her grandmother and other family members had been involved in occultic practices. There was also sexual lust in the family line. These witchcraft spirits from her exposure to transcendental meditation made her fear and dislike of men greater, and were the primary cause of her lustful dreams. She needed deliverance from these spirits and much inner healing.

I broke the generational curse of occultism and lust with powerful spiritual warfare in the mighty name of Jesus. I also had her picture herself standing behind the cross, and her parents in front of the cross. I had her see the generational curses of her family line stopping at the cross, to see them on Jesus — who, as we have seen, became a curse for us. You can do this same thing.

Laugh and Cry Your Way to Freedom

As a child, Phyliss' father had ignored her for the most part, giving her little affection. She got along poorly with her mother. This caused a deep wounding in her spirit and required much inner healing.

Phyliss described later to me how this ministry to her had changed her life. "I can now cry before the Lord," she said, "and feel His presence deeply. The Lord has become my Friend. I am able to make friends with others more easily, I am free of lustful dreams, and my fear of men is totally gone."

Virginia: Hindrances Removed

Because of her inability to speak freely in tongues, Virginia's prayer life had been limited, as well as her ability to open up to the gifts of *"prophecy," "divers kinds of tongues,"* and the accompanying gift of *"interpretation of tongues"* (1 Corinthians 12:8-10). She and her family had been involved in the New Age movement, causing her to be bound by a number of evil spirits. We prayed a strong prayer of deliverance over her, breaking the generational curse of this involvement. We then commanded those spirits, in Jesus' name, to release her so she could speak freely in tongues. Something broke inside of her, and a flow of tongues began to come forth. Tongues flowed, joy flowed and even laughter came as the Holy Spirit set Virginia free.

Many Christians cannot pray freely in tongues because of an evil spirit blocking them. You too can be set free. Let the Lord do it for you. Fight the good fight of faith. Come boldly to the throne of grace.

Breaking the Power of Generational Iniquity
Continuing Freedom

The happy ending to these stories doesn't mean that these people never again had a need for more inner healing or deliverance. Because of the great victory God had given me through deliverance from occultic spirits, I thought I was totally free. I was incredibly changed and blessed. I was to learn, however, that I was only partially delivered and needed further releases from the occultic exposure and other generational curses. As I received more and more from the Lord, I gained more freedom, more peace and a greater closeness to Jesus and to my loved ones.

Several years ago, as I was meditating on generational iniquity, the Lord revealed a surprising and immensely important truth to me. He showed me that even when we have had much deliverance from generational curses, the deliverance is rarely more than ten to twenty-five percent complete. Later, the Lord expounded on this revelation and showed me that this ten to twenty-five percent principle applies in many other areas, including inner healing and deliverance from negative soul ties, from inner vows, and from financial curses.

Whenever God reveals truth, it is to bless us and to set us free, never to condemn us. If we will cooperate with the Holy Spirit, what sounds like bad news can become good news. The truth is that all of us have the need of much more inner healing and deliverance — much of it involving generational curses. Such curses are often the root cause of one or more big problems in our lives. God has a mighty provision for setting us free through the shed blood of Christ and by the power of the Holy Spirit.

Laugh and Cry Your Way to Freedom

We all walk in much denial, and facing these truths can be painful. If we are willing, however, it can lead to beautiful changes in our lives. May each of us be willing to face the truth about our need for inner healing and much more inner sanctification. Those bad attitudes, the occasional curse word, the lustful thoughts, the unclean dreams — let us look at them as THE TIP OF THE ICEBERG of much inner darkness. And keep in mind, again, that an important root of every weakness, every sin and every bad attitude is in our generational inheritance.

Wonderful new releases and victories are coming your way, but these victories are not automatic. You must know the truth, so that you can be set free. You can be liberated to face the future in a whole new dimension of fulfillment.

Focused and Fervent Prayers

When you are praying to break free from generational curses, your prayers must be pinpointed, or focused, in specific areas of exposure. Focused prayers get answers. This applies to each area of the occult you may have been in or been influenced by. For example, recently the Lord was having me do spiritual warfare in specific areas of the occult to which I had been exposed — my use of the ouïja board and of the pendulum, water dowsing or witching, going once to a fortune-teller, and dabbling in hypnotism. I had to pray hard in each area separately, with much groaning in the Spirit (self-travail). In fact, you will usually need to pray several times in each area to get the complete release, the complete victory.

As I lay on my face before the Lord, He showed me much

Breaking the Power of Generational Iniquity

occultism from my mother's side of the family, and some from my father's side. I have prayed for long periods, with much spiritual warfare and self-travail, and have had tremendous breakthroughs. Prayer is hard work, and we need to pray until we get the assurance in our spirit that we have the victory. This is known as "praying through."

Be sure you are specific in your prayers. If you know that your grandmother, your uncle and your great-grandfather were into the occult, then forgive each of them separately for this negative inheritance. Pray much in tongues and, preferably, in self-travail until you know the forgiveness is real, not just mental. It is also important to repent for all your relatives involved in the occult, unto the third and fourth generation. This type of prayer is known as "identification repentance," a frequent Old Testament prayer method.

Next, in Jesus' name, you must break the power of the spirits affecting you from each of these family members. When possible, take family members one at a time, not as a group. Do this also for the generational curses in other areas, such as lust, alcoholism, depression and fear.

You must not ask God to make the devil leave. In Jesus' name, you must take authority over him and break his power. You must command him to leave. Jesus proclaimed:

> *And I will give unto THEE the keys of the kingdom of heaven: and whatsoever THOU shalt bind on earth shall be bound in heaven: and whatsoever THOU shalt loose on earth shall be loosed in heaven.*
> Matthew 16:19

Laugh and Cry Your Way to Freedom

Submit yourselves therefore to God. Resist the devil, and he will flee from you. James 4:7

Jesus has given you the authority to bind Satan, to break his power — so do it! Weak, little, religious or complaining prayers will not accomplish anything. Your prayers must be passionate and they must be intense. As the Scriptures declared:

The effectual fervent prayer of a righteous man availeth much. James 5:16

Satanic Appointments vs Divine Appointments

When your parents have been involved in seances, astrology, tarot card reading or other forms of witchcraft, it opens you up to destructive satanic appointments. It brings the wrong people and negative circumstances into your life. The very person who will be a curse in your life will be drawn to you. Strange accidents will happen to you.

This is about to change completely. The Father has a plan of total victory for you. He has many divine appointments of His own with which to bless you, and others through you.

It may take many sessions of deep prayer with much warfare, and probably much self-travail, but the time will come when you will know that you have prayed through completely. The Lord will give you an assurance within, a peace that you have obtained complete victory in a particular area.

Breaking the Power of Generational Iniquity

The Open Doors to Your Soul

You may not think that your exposure to the occult has been sufficient to merit such drastic action in prayer. After all, you only played with the ouïja board once or twice. You were only in one seance. Your interest in astrology and ESP was only passing. And you can't understand how you could have been affected by listening to rock music. When a door has been opened into your soul, however, evil spirits can enter until the door is shut. No wonder such involvement causes serious problems in the areas of sexual lust, money and power!

Probably seventy-five percent or more of us have been directly exposed to the occult, and have a great need for these doors to be closed. How can you close those doors? First, break the power of witchcraft in your family line through much spiritual warfare. Then command, in Jesus' name, that those doors be closed, and do much praying in tongues in spiritual warfare.

Pray with authority. The Lord will give you an assurance when the doors are completely closed. With your eyes closed, if you ask Him, the Holy Spirit will often show you by vision whether or not the doors are closed. Pray until you get that assurance.

Conclusion

As we have observed, the generational curse from occultism is only one of many areas of generational iniquity that need to be broken. We must also focus our spiritual warfare on other areas of generational iniquity, such as depression, alcoholism, lust, nervousness, abusiveness, dishonesty, divorce and poverty. We inherit numerous curses from our family line. All such inherited curses should be dealt with individually, not as a group. For example, if your mother suffered much depression, you probably will be attacked in this area also. See the cross of Jesus between you and your mother stopping that spirit of depression. Boldly claim it as done in the name of Jesus, and do much spiritual warfare about it, letting the Holy Spirit intercede for you, by praying in tongues.

Also, with tears, deeply forgive your mother for childhood rejection and other hurts. Deep forgiveness of parents through inner healing is the most important key to being released completely from generational curses.

God's will, and His great desire, is to set us totally free from every negative effect of generational iniquity. Learning just a few of the Holy Spirit methods in this chapter will benefit you immensely and enable you to be free and to help free others. Use these powerful Holy Spirit methods of being set free — *Laugh and Cry Your Way to Freedom.*

Chapter 8

Breaking the Power of Destructive Inner Vows

Swear not at all ... . But let your communication be, Yea, yea; Nay, nay: for whatsoever is more than these cometh of evil. Matthew 5:34-37

The word *swear* means "to vow, to promise, to affirm, or to confess." Unless vows are inspired by the Holy Spirit, they can produce great harm in our lives. Vows made in childhood, often long forgotten, are the most harmful and often have far-reaching and devastating effects on individuals throughout their lives.

Janet: "I Will Never Let Myself Be Hurt Again"

For most of our meeting, Janet sat expressionless, with a blank, hollow look on her face. She had been an emotionally and sexually abused child, rejected by her father and given very little love by her mother. As a result, little

Janet made a decision deep within her heart, an inner vow, that she would never allow anyone to hurt her again. She accomplished this by refusing to give or to receive love. As an adult, Janet was locked into a self-made prison, held in bondage by this inner vow not to be hurt, not to love, and not to let people get to know her.

Now thirty years old, Janet came to our meeting in desperation, feeling she could not go on living without an inner healing miracle from God. The pain within her heart was overwhelming. She was unable to establish a close relationship with anyone. As a result, she had no real friends and had never married.

We explained to Janet that she would need to break the childhood inner vow, which had protected her from hurts for so many years, because it was now destroying her. Her inner vow, which had been a wall of protection, had become a prison. Many people are in that same prison because of an inner vow made in childhood. You may be one of them. I was.

Breaking the Inner Vow — Coming Out of Prison

We asked Janet if she was willing to break the inner vow, and she said, "Oh, yes." We next asked her if she was willing to forgive her father, her mother and the sexual abuser. She quickly affirmed her willingness. "Yes, yes, yes," she said, "I can't go on any longer as I am." She made the decision to become vulnerable, to begin to trust people.

Next, we took her through a prayer of forgiveness and a long blessing prayer for her father, for her mother, and then for the sexual abuser. We then proceeded, in the mighty name of Jesus, to have her do spiritual warfare in loud tongues and even in holy laughter. After a few minutes, she felt a great release come. The inner vow was broken!

Next, we prayed for more holy laughter to come upon Janet. She laughed and laughed and laughed. From the holy laughter came a release of much rage and healing of the pain-filled childhood years — the root cause of her inner vow being made. Suddenly, Janet exclaimed, "My face has become unfrozen! My face has become unfrozen! It felt stiff before! I'm a new person!"

She continued to rejoice, saying, "I'm free! I'm free! I'm free!" She had been released from the "prison" in which the inner vow had placed her.

Childhood Inner Vows

It is estimated that about twenty-five per cent of women are molested sexually in childhood by family members or others, and nearly all of these women make a strong inner vow to shut down their emotions and to distrust all men (and this often includes God). Because of this, relationships with other people are doomed to failure, and a happy and fulfilling marriage becomes almost impossible.

The deep desire to protect oneself from further hurt causes many to make inner vows in childhood. An inner vow like Janet's, not to be hurt again, is one of those most frequently made. For many of us, such a vow is powerful and prevents us from becoming vulnerable and transparent in our relationships with others. It keeps "the real me" from being seen or known by others. Such inner vows become the root cause of our having a distrust of men, of women, of preachers, or of others. Three of the most damaging inner vows are "I won't trust anyone," "I won't show my emotions," and "To be loved, I must earn it."

A Vow to Suppress Our Emotions

When we make a vow to suppress our emotions, it holds us back from childlikeness, from being the person God has created us to be, and from loving and receiving love in the dimension that the Lord has for us. Moreover, it bottles up the rivers of living water, making it difficult to teach, preach, witness or prophesy with the freedom the Lord desires. It also hinders our ability to praise and worship God with the intensity and fullness He desires.

Make a decision, in Jesus' name, to break any inner vows you may have made, and then, in spiritual warfare, shout in tongues for two or three minutes. To break the vow deeply and to open up to the "rivers of living waters" shout in tongues for thirty minutes a day for three days in a row. Many have testified that this changed their lives, and your life will be changed too, as a result of your obedience.

My Inner Vow

When I was about twelve, my parents transferred me from a public school to a private one. I was warned that it might be difficult for me to attain even passing grades. To make matters worse, I was being separated from all of my old friends.

I fiercely determined to do well. I overzealously sought to be outstanding in my grades, and this offended many of my new peers. To everyone's surprise, including my own, I made the highest grades in my class. This led to jealousy, criticism and rejection from the other students, and that, of course, hurt me deeply.

This whole affair came to the attention of the principal, and one day he called me into his office. He criticized me for my extreme "eagerness" in pursuing excellence. He was probably right, but what he said that day hurt me deeply, and I made an inner vow that I would no longer seek excellence.

In spite of many natural talents and much hard studying, I never again made the honor roll — in middle school, high school, college or graduate school. And I could not understand why. That inner vow had become a curse on my life. My ability to be excellent was imprisoned. That vow also negatively affected many other areas of my life, such as business, hobbies, sports and personal relationships.

A few years ago the Lord revealed to me that I had made this damaging inner vow. Since then the Holy Spirit has led me to spend much time breaking it through spiritual warfare, including the deep groanings of self-travail. Over and over I have confessed spiritual truths about being excellent for God, such as *"I am more than a conqueror through Christ Jesus"* and *"I can do all things through Christ who strengtheneth me."* I thank God that Jesus loved me so much that He became a curse for me so that I could be free. The vow has lost its power over me. I am free to be excellent for the Lord. I too have come out of prison.

Rose: Still Sucking Her Thumb at Twelve

Negative vows we make in later life also hurt us, but an

inner vow is one that is usually established in us in childhood. It is usually forgotten, but it continues to exert a powerful influence over our lives.

Rose was still sucking her thumb at the age of twelve. She came to us in despair. Her friends made fun of her. In spite of a great effort on her part, she could not break the habit.

The Lord revealed to us that, at age two, she had made an inner vow not to grow up. With our encouragement, she made the decision that she wanted to grow up and that she would not remain a little girl any longer. With her permission, we then broke that vow in the powerful name of Jesus. We also included a long prayer for the Lord Jesus to "grow her up" to her present age of twelve.

Rose lost all desire to suck her thumb. During the next several weeks, we saw her many times, and she was still free and experiencing an amazing growth in maturity. She had "grown up" to age twelve.

The vow not to grow up is one that a great percentage of us make. Each of us needs to express a willingness to God to grow up, and then do spiritual warfare to break this vow.

Rose, Janet, and I were dramatically changed by breaking an inner vow. Is it possible that your life also can be changed by doing the same? Do you need to come out of your self-made prison?

Earned Love vs Unconditional Love

God loves us unconditionally, just as we are, and not

Breaking the Power of Destructive Inner Vows

because of how much we pray, read His Word, fast, give or attend church. We likewise should love our children unconditionally. We should love them because they are our children and not because of what they do or become.

In most homes, however, love is given on the basis of who has earned it. If you have made an inner vow that you must earn love to be loved, you will find yourself continually striving to be good enough, to be worthy enough, for people to love you — even to be loved by God. Usually you will never feel quite good enough.

Most of us have made this inner vow, or affirmation, that we must earn love, and it is very damaging to our interpersonal relationships. First of all, such a vow causes children to strive for good grades, success in sports, music, or in other ways, to "earn" love from their parents. Secondly, once they have reached the teenage years, to be accepted by their peers, many start using drugs, having sex and rejecting God. And striving to earn love is not just a teenage problem. It carries over into later life.

Those who have this problem never feel worthy unless they are constantly doing things for others. This vow needs to be broken in the mighty name of Jesus, and our minds need to be renewed to the truth of God's unconditional love. We are made worthy only by the blood of Christ.

Conclusion

In conclusion, inner vows cause many problems in our relationships with others and with God. Freedom from them is often the key to major releases. Seek the Lord for a revelation of destructive inner vows in your life, and then break them just as Janet, Rose and I did. This will lead to major, even life-transforming, changes in your life. Breaking these destructive inner vows will help you to be *Changed Into His Image Through Inner Healing.*"

Chapter 9

Negative Soul Ties, Idolatry and Fragmentation

They are all estranged from me through their idols. ... Repent, and turn yourselves from your idols; and turn away your faces from all your abominations.
Ezekiel 14:5-6

Mental, emotional or physical abuse from key people in our lives causes injurious, often hate-filled, negative soul ties. Such soul ties and the abuse or rejection that causes them also cause a fragmentation, ripping or tearing of one's heart. It is as though part of our heart is missing. Negative soul ties need to be broken through strong spiritual warfare, and we must be healed from the effects of fragmentation.

Alice: An Unhealthy Attraction

Alice pleaded with us, "I want to discontinue the relationship, but I feel an unhealthy and unwanted attraction to him. I don't seem to have the will to break away. Please help me to be free!"

For several years, Alice, a lovely black sister, had a male telephone prayer partner. God consistently answered the prayers the two of them prayed together, and for a year or two, it had been a fulfilling and fruitful relationship. Gradually, however, the man had beocame more and more controlling. Also, Alice had discovered sexual uncleanness and dishonesty in his life. In the process of their praying together, their souls had become tied together with invisible chains. Now, Alice found herself unable to break free, and she was crying to God and to us for help.

The first thing Pattie and I did was ask her if she was willing to forgive her prayer partner for his dishonesty, his uncleanness and his controlling methods. Forgiveness is essential to being set free from such soul ties. She indicated that she was willing to do so. We then led her through a prayer of forgiveness for the man. This included praying a long prayer of blessing over him, a sincere "blessing prayer," because God commands us to bless our *"enemies."*

Next, we had Alice pray loudly in tongues. Then, we asked her if she was willing to laugh about the hurts. Laughter, as we have seen, produces inner healing, removes much emotional pain and also weakens the negative soul tie. She said she was willing to laugh in the Spirit.

As Alice was praying loudly in tongues, we laid hands on her for holy laughter. She laughed, laughed and laughed some more, and soon she broke into deep sobbing for heartfelt emotional pains. She was undergoing deep self-travail, which, as we have seen, is the key to deep and quick inner healing. After a short time of this travail, a deep peace came into her heart.

Now Alice was ready to break the soul tie with her prayer partner. A negative soul tie often opens one to an oppressing evil spirit, so we almost always have those seeking deliverance do spiritual warfare through speaking in tongues and through "pleading the blood of Jesus" (invoking the power of the blood) over the soul tie.

We also used an unusual method which the Holy Spirit has given us (and probably others). The secret of it is found in the book of Hebrews:

> *For the word of God is quick, and powerful, and sharper than any two-edged sword, piercing even to the dividing asunder of soul and spirit.*
> Hebrews 4:12

Somewhat as a prophetic act, we have individuals take *"the sword of the Spirit"* in their hands and viciously cut the soul tie, usually doing warfare in tongues at the same time. We had Alice do this, and soon the soul tie was completely severed.

Next, in the name of Jesus, we commanded the "missing part of Alice's heart" to return. We instructed her to pray: "In Jesus' name, I command the missing part of my heart to return now."

I then said to Alice, "Now take a deep breath (representing the breath, or life, of God), and receive back the missing part of your heart."

Alice did this twice, and soon she felt a great peace, her pains from arthritis evaporated and the oppressing spirits she had battled for over a year were gone. "I feel a great release and peace deep within me," she said. "I feel free." Alice was set free, and you can be, too!

Negative Soul Ties and Idolatry

We are created in need of an intimate relationship with God. When we fail to have a close relationship with Him, we try to fill the void through relationships of various types with people. In doing that, we often develop negative soul ties with some of them.

We also sometimes attempt to fill the void in our lives with things, such as hobbies, sports, alcohol, drugs, sex, pornography, soap operas and even church. This is idolatry, giving to "things" the worship, loyalty or priority which belongs to God.

When we develop harmful soul ties with individuals, we give to them part of our heart or love that should be reserved for God or for others. For example, a strong negative soul tie with a prayer partner can rob our spouse or our children of affection due to them.

We also can pick up negative traits and evil spirits from our soul ties. We thus are often controlled by other people through such negative soul ties, or by things (idolatry), and are not free to love and be loved in a healthy, godly way. These soul ties need to be broken.

The Damage Caused by Fragmentation

We need to focus on breaking the most damaging, stron-

Negative Soul Ties, Idolatry and Fragmentation

gest soul ties, because these cause a great fragmentation of our hearts. These soul ties usually come from:

1. Childhood mental, emotional or physical abuse by our parents or by other important authority figures in our lives, or from childhood sexual abuse by our parents or others. Emotional abuse includes possessive, controlling or smothering love.
2. Ex-husbands, ex-wives or ex-lovers.
3. Anyone in our lives controlling us, or our controlling them.
4. Any person with whom we had a deep relationship who was involved in the occult. Such occultic soul ties always result in serious fragmentation of the heart.
5. A spiritual leader, such as a pastor or an evangelist, who has hurt us badly or whom we idolize.
6. A church denomination or a cult or even other Christians.
7. Aborted children.
8. Deceased loved ones, if we are still grieving or have been deeply hurt by them.

Childhood Hurts and Negative Soul Ties

In childhood, we develop a strong bonding to our parents. Some of this is good and pleasing to the Lord, but much of it is of a negative nature because of the mistakes they make in raising us. No matter how good you think your childhood was, most likely you have many forgotten or deeply buried hurts from your past. You may have received very little love, or conditional or possessive love. Some of our parents were alcoholics; some had deep emotional or even mental problems. A large number of us have been abused verbally, emotionally and even sexually by one or both of our parents.

Often we identify being loved with earning love by our accomplishments. We feel we must earn love by doing good things or by being a "good" person.

Our emotional pain leads to unforgiveness, bitterness and enormous amounts of rage toward our parents and, later in life, toward others. This causes us to develop strong negative soul ties with our parents, and through these soul ties, we take on their negative qualities, becoming more and more like them. Although many children of alcoholic parents vow that they will NEVER be like their alcoholic parents, the fact is that a great majority of the children of alcoholic parents either become alcoholics or workaholics themselves or marry someone who is.

Those who were abused sexually as children vow that they will protect their children from being abused in that same way, but the fact is that many of those who were themselves sexually abused as children end up doing the same things to their own children or marrying someone who does.

The good news is that Jesus, on the cross of Calvary, has purchased victory for you and me from all negative soul ties and their harmful effects. It comes through forgiveness, inner healing and deliverance.

These childhood hurts also blind us to truth. We see our parents' negative qualities in God, in our spouses, and in others. This, in turn, causes us to distrust God and everyone else.

Negative Soul Ties, Idolatry and Fragmentation

Your deep forgiveness of your parents and breaking the negative soul ties with them sets you free to establish healthy relationships with others. If you are married, it enables you to *"leave"* your parents and to *"cleave"* to your spouse — to be one in spirit, soul and body with him or her.

Sharon: Grief From Mother's Death

Your body can be deeply affected by negative emotions, such as bitterness, fear and grief. These harmful emotions can cause or contribute to arthritis, migraine headaches, cancer, stress and depression.

Shortly after her mother's death, Sharon developed severe chest pains, which continued for five long years. She and her mother had been close, and her mother's death had been a great heartache for her, physically and emotionally. Furthermore, Sharon wasn't willing or able to "let her mother go." This resulted in a strong soul tie with her mother that needed to be broken — if Sharon was to be free from the resultant grief.

Like Sharon, most of us still carry an enormous amount of hidden grief from the death of loved ones. Such grief usually includes a combination of rage, guilt feelings and loneliness from the loss. For example, after twenty years I still had grief over the death of my mother, my father and my grandmother. I still had a soul tie with them that needed to be broken. In recent years, through the *"groanings,"* the self-travail, of Romans 8:26, the Lord has set me free from these soul ties as well as from the grief, and with these releases He has brought a new peace into my life. He will do the same for you.

Laugh and Cry Your Way to Freedom

We asked Sharon if she was willing to forgive her mother for dying. That may seem like a strange question to many. We have found, however, that most of us have not forgiven our loved ones for dying. We resent their leaving us here alone because we need them.

Sharon was willing to forgive, so we took her through a prayer of forgiveness. We then had her laugh repeatedly (with holy laughter) at the pain of losing her mother. She both laughed and cried until peace came.

As with Alice, we also had Sharon take the sword of the Spirit and cut the soul tie with her deceased mother. We also had her call back the missing, fragmented part of her heart given to her mother. When we asked, "Sharon, how do you feel?" she replied, "I feel whole on the inside. I feel wonderful."

No prayer had been offered for the healing of the severe chest pains, but none was needed. They were gone. She was totally healed of that condition.

We have a great and awesome God, who does all things well. You can be liberated from existing soul ties with deceased loved ones. You can be free from grief. God wants your life to be one of righteousness, peace and joy.

A Husband and Wife: Both Delivered

A woman was grieving deeply over the death of her father who had died seven years earlier. I laid hands upon her and ministered to her, and she travailed deeply before the Lord. She was totally set free from the soul tie with her father and from the deep pain of her father's death. A new joy came into her life. Her husband, who

Negative Soul Ties, Idolatry and Fragmentation

was sitting beside her, then became aware of the deep sorrow he still had over his father's death three years before. He requested prayer, and he too was wonderfully delivered into a new joy. How about you?

Establishing Godly Soul Ties With Your Marriage Partner

Jesus taught:

> *A man shall leave father and mother, and shall cleave to his wife: and they twain shall be one flesh. Wherefore they are no more twain, but one flesh.*
> Matthew 19:5-6

What does "leaving" your parents mean. It primarily means being set free from overdependence on your parents — emotionally, financially or spiritually. This involves breaking negative soul ties with them. "Leaving" applies to both husband and wife, and this separation, this breaking of negative soul ties, includes ex-spouses, ex-lovers and even some of your close friends.

This doesn't mean that you should give up good friends or that you are being disloyal to your parents. When God sets you free from negative soul ties and heals you of fragmentation, you will have a more healthy relationship with your parents, your friends and your spouse.

Your first loyalty should now be to your wife or husband. There must be no running back and forth to Mother or Dad — either in person, by telephone, or emotionally. The negative soul tie, the negative emotional bonding with your parents, must be completely broken. You must "leave" them so that you can "cleave" to your spouse. This is the only way you can become truly one flesh with your spouse — united in spirit, soul and body. You will now be joined to your marriage partner with a greatly beneficial, godly soul tie.

Correct Priorities

You must never put your children before your spouse. This includes children from a previous marriage (although you must love them and protect them from an abusive marriage partner). God must be first in your life, your marriage partner second, your children third, your job fourth and your ministry fifth. If your priorities are right, you will have a dynamic, successful ministry, whether as an interceding housewife, a witnessing plumber or a big-name evangelist.

Soul Ties: New Converts and Hungry Christians

For those of you who are new Christians (or for older Christians who desire to be greatly used of God), God wants you to break those soul ties with your former drinking, gambling or even fishing buddies. Unless these individuals become truly converted and sold-out to Jesus, they will be a bad influence on you. Your old habits still have power to pull you back into the "prison" of sin. You should not even enjoy being with those worldly companions. You are a new person in Christ.

You need to become a member of a dynamic Christian

Negative Soul Ties, Idolatry and Fragmentation

church where the Word of God is preached and the power of God is present. You need to find new friends who love Jesus and think and act like you do.

It may even be hard to spend time with certain family members who live, talk and think differently from the "new you." Their company will pull you down:

> *Wherefore come out from among them, and be ye separate, saith the Lord, and touch not the unclean thing ... and ye shall be my sons and daughters, saith the Lord Almighty.*   2 Corinthians 6:17-18

God is calling all of us to walk in intimacy with Him. What a blessing! What a privilege!

Marilyn: Grief for a Dead Son

Marilyn's son had been dead for five years. She loved her husband and the Lord, but she was in continual emotional pain over the son's death. The deep grief over her son's death and her unwillingness to "let him go" had caused an injurious soul tie with him. Her husband said, "Since our son's death, no one has been able to help Marilyn. She is not able to function as a wife or as a mother. I hope you can help her."

Marilyn was also tormented by having been sexually abused by her father and uncle as a little girl. This sexual abuse had caused great shame and emotional pain, which led to a negative, damaging soul tie with each of them. Because of these soul ties established as a child, all the emotional pain that accompanied them and the trauma of the death of her son, Marilyn was emotionally crippled. Through these harmful soul ties, she was emotionally chained to the three of them.

Marilyn expressed her willingness to forgive her father and her uncle, and as I said before, this is an important step to being set free from harmful soul ties. Pattie and I then asked her to pray a prayer of forgiveness and a special prayer of requesting the Lord to bless her *"enemies,"* those who had abused her. We then ministered further inner healing to her for this terrible abuse caused by her father and uncle.

After about thirty minutes of inner healing prayer for the wounds she had suffered from her father and uncle, we next broke the negative soul ties with each of them. As these soul tie chains were broken, a tremendous release took place within Marilyn.

Next, Marilyn was ready for the healing of her fragmented, torn heart caused by both the sexual abuse and the loss of her son. She was ready to "call back" the missing parts of her heart, given or taken by her father and uncle. We did this in the name of Jesus, and a wonderful restoration of her heart took place.

Marilyn was now ready for the emotional healing and breaking of the negative soul tie with her son. After about fifteen minutes of inner healing for the pain of losing her son, with her permission and cooperation, we broke the soul tie with her deceased son, releasing her son to Jesus.

When loved ones die, they take with them part of our hearts. Special ministry was needed for Marilyn's fragmented, torn heart to be made whole. We called back into her heart the portion given to her deceased son.

Negative Soul Ties, Idolatry and Fragmentation

"How do you feel, Marilyn?" we enquired.

"Words cannot describe how I feel," replied Marilyn. She continued, "My husband won't recognize me. I'm a new person. I feel so free, and I feel such a deep peace."

She indeed left a new person. Her husband had a new wife, and her children had a new mother.

Lily: Scarred by Sexual Abuse

We live in a society where teenage sex is becoming commonplace among non-Christians and even among many Christians. Pattie and I have discovered that when teenage girls are sexually involved with several boys, in the vast majority of cases, these girls have been molested sexually as children. For them to be free, the soul ties with their abusers need to be broken. This is what happened with Lily.

Lily had been badly scarred by frequent sexual abuse by her brother. A strong spirit of lust had been transferred to her from him, so that during her teenage years she'd had sexual affairs, mostly abusive, with many young men, establishing soul ties with each of them. Lily was now married and loved her husband — as much as she was able to love. Much of her heart was actually missing because of previous "lovers." She had given each of them part of her heart. Her heart was deeply fragmented.

Early in their marriage, Lily and her husband both became Spirit-filled Christians, but she still found herself with lustful thoughts and desires for others. She cried out to God for deliverance.

Pattie and I first ministered to Lily for deep hurts and

rejection from both parents. Soon she fell out under the power of God onto His "operating table." She cried and laughed, and then came more deep crying for these childhood pains. Under the anointing of the Spirit, we always intersperse these prayers with holy laughter. As we have seen, such laughter produces inner healing and is a powerful tool in spiritual warfare. Sometimes self-pity can begin to come into self-travail, but holy laughter will quickly remove it.

Next on the Holy Spirit's agenda was to minister to Lily to be free from the shame and the deep scars of her sexual abuse from her brother. She was willing to forgive him. After this prayer of forgiveness, we had her shout loudly in tongues. Then we laid hands on her for holy laughter for the sexual abuse. This is, as we have seen, a powerful spiritual tool for freeing Christians from horrible experiences or fears.

God's powerful, life-changing truths are usually simple. Use this powerful tool of holy laughter in your life and in ministering to others. It helps to produce deep inner healing, and it triggers self-travail — the groanings, sobbing and crying of Romans 8:26.

As we laid hands on her, Lily immediately began laughing in the Spirit uproariously about the sexual abuse. This holy laughter continued for quite a while, and then she began sobbing in self-travail, producing much inner healing and cleansing. This also caused the beginning of deliverance from evil spirits of lust and rage.

I could sense in the Spirit, by the word of knowledge, that she had deep screams of rage within her. I told Lily the Lord desired her to scream when I laid hands on her. I

Negative Soul Ties, Idolatry and Fragmentation

assured her the Lord would anoint it! She agreed, and under the anointing of the Holy Spirit, she screamed and screamed and screamed. This released immense quantities of rage from within her and led to further deep inner healing. Such anointed screaming, sobbing, mourning or groaning is a spiritual method the Holy Spirit uses to produce deliverance, cleansing and inner healing.

The Word of God says:

> *Be afflicted, and MOURN, and weep: let your laughter be turned to MOURNING, and your joy to heaviness.* James 4:9

> *Likewise the Spirit also helpeth our infirmities: for we know not what we should pray for as we ought: but the Spirit itself maketh intercession for us with GROANINGS which cannot be uttered.*
> Romans 8:26

Because of the fear of seeming fanatical, it took me months to get up the courage to tell people to scream in the Spirit. Now it seems so normal. Screams have always taken place in times of great revival, during times of deep travail by Christians, and when the fire of God has come upon individuals.

Many of us are full of screams we have buried within us over the years. The Lord wants us to give Him these ashes of our lives that He may give us His beauty and wholeness.

After this, the Holy Spirit led us to lay hands on Lily for more holy laughter. We repeated this Spirit-led procedure several times until we felt the victory in our spirits. The Lord healed her deeply from her childhood sexual abuse.

With much spiritual warfare, we then broke the soul tie with her brother. Next, we "called back" into her heart the missing part "taken" by her brother through his abuse and control.

In the name of Jesus we broke the soul ties Lily had formed with each of these young men she had sex with as a teenager and "called back" the missing part of her heart given to them or "taken" by them.

About three weeks later we received a letter from Lily. She wrote: "My life has taken on new meaning. I am in love with Jesus, and I know He's in love with me. My prayer life is awesome because I really know that I am in His presence. ... God has really called me to a ministry of intercession through travail and self-travail. Oh, yes ... I am now able to love my husband because I have a whole heart."

Isn't that wonderful! Our Father, through His Son Jesus, does all things well. He will do it for you also. You, too, can laugh your way to freedom.

James: An Illicit Soul Tie Leads to Greater Sin

James was the pastor of a thriving church with about three hundred faithful members. His work load was heavy, and he didn't find much time to be with his family. His wife was hard to communicate with and didn't understand him. His highly efficient, lovely church secretary did communicate deeply with him. He was able to share so much with her, things his wife didn't seem to understand. He

Negative Soul Ties, Idolatry and Fragmentation

therefore began to share with her more and more the burdens on his heart that should have been shared only with his wife. This is known as spiritual adultery, and it usually leads to the forming of a strong negative soul tie between the two individuals. It also often leads to natural adultery.

Like most pastors, James overworked, didn't spend enough time with the Lord or with his family, and needed deliverance from a spirit of lust (a problem with almost all men). A soul tie was being established with his secretary. She was a lonely person and was drawn to him. Soon they found themselves in an adulterous affair.

James loved his wife, his three lovely children and his church, but when he was advised to break off the affair and get rid of his secretary or he would lose everything, his reply was, "I can't do it. She is life to me." A powerful soul tie, including a spirit of lust, had gripped him so tightly that he didn't see how he could be free of it. It had a grip not only on his emotions, but also on his thinking.

James was deceived. He was sure this woman was life to him, when in fact she was death. Sin is like that. It promises life, but brings death:

> *For the wages of sin is death; but the gift of God is eternal life through Jesus Christ our Lord.*
> Romans 6:23

Because sin had such a strong hold on James, he lost his wife, his children and his church. This same tragedy is being acted out far too often in the lives of pastors, evangelists and other Christians leaders in every part of the world. Marriages, ministries, careers and sometimes eternal destinies are being destroyed, and no one seems to know what to do about it.

How can these tragedies be prevented? And how can they be healed when they do happen? Understanding the need for deliverance from a spirit of lust and understanding the evil nature of spiritual adultery and the resulting soul ties is a big step.

Conclusion

Jesus has come for restoration. His work is:

> *... to heal the brokenhearted, to preach deliverance to the captives, and recovering of sight to the blind, to set at liberty them that are bruised.* Luke 4:18

We all have many unhealed hurts, unrevealed sin, negative soul ties and fragmented hearts. The good news is that you can be set free just as Lily, Alice, Marilyn and countless others have been. Using just a few of the simple Holy Spirit methods or tools discussed in this chapter will bring tremendous releases into your life and, through you, into the lives of others. You need to *Laugh and Cry Your Way to Freedom*.

Chapter 10

The Renewed Mind and Inner Healing

And be not conformed to this world: but be ye transformed by the renewing of your mind, that ye may prove what is that good, and acceptable, and perfect, will of God.   Romans 12:2

For to be carnally minded is death; but to be spiritually minded is life and peace.   Romans 8:6

For as he thinketh in his heart, so is he.
              Proverbs 23:7

When you say "I can't," you are right, even if you are a child of God. When you say "I can't," you are siding with the devil against the Word of God, and you will not be able to accomplish the things God desires in your life! When you repeatedly state, *"I can do all things through Christ which strengtheneth me"* (Philippians 4:13), then you can do them because the wisdom and power of God will be with you. There is tremendous power in the way we think and the words that we choose to express our thoughts.

You cannot have a negative mind and a victorious life. A life with ungodly beliefs and a life of victory cannot go together. When we side with the devil against God's Word, we are in big trouble!

> *Death and life are in the power of the tongue: and they that love it shall eat the fruit thereof.*
> Proverbs 18:21

We must cast down all negative thoughts that the devil brings to our minds and replace them with faith thoughts. We must fight the good fight of faith. There is tremendous victory in having our minds in agreement with God's Word. This is what faith is: believing and taking action on God's Word, on His promises.

We need not be victims of the past, nor of people, nor of present circumstances. The Lord is our Shepherd. Trust Him and His promises. He will never leave you nor forsake you. Let Him be in control of your life.

We must renew our minds to the truths that we can, indeed, do all things through our mighty Lord Jesus, and that in every difficulty, God will be the source of supplying all of our needs. The Scriptures promise:

> *We are more than conquerors through him that loved us.*
> Romans 8:37

> *But my God shall supply all your need according to his riches in glory by Christ Jesus.*
> Philippians 4:19

The Renewed Mind and Inner Healing

These truths will mightily change your life.

When you believe that through Jesus Christ you can be successful in every area of your life, God will bring it to pass (see Psalm 37:5). When you disbelieve or doubt, you attract "reasons" and negative people to support your disbelief. Doubt, disbelief and a subconscious will to fail, the not-really-wanting-to-succeed mentality, is responsible for most failures. This is a demonic stronghold that needs to be broken through the renewal of your mind.

Moving From Darkness Into Light

What does it mean, then, to have your mind renewed, and what will it accomplish for you? It is a complete change in the way you view life and relationships. It is moving from darkness into light, from the natural or carnal way of thinking to the spiritual. To have a "renewed mind" means to have the way you think changed by the Holy Spirit to the way God thinks and believes. You begin to see things from God's perspective, from His viewpoint. He has said:

> *My thoughts are not your thoughts, neither are your ways my ways, saith the* L<small>ORD</small>*. For as the heavens are higher than the earth, so are my ways higher than your ways, and my thoughts than your thoughts.*
> Isaiah 55:8-9

Faith in God — in His truth, in His principles — will become a way of life. You will experience and live in the peace that passes all understanding.

Laugh and Cry Your Way to Freedom

The way you think will affect your words and your actions and, therefore, will determine whether you live in victory or defeat, in fulfillment or frustration.

> *A good man out of the good treasure of the heart bringeth forth good things: and an evil man out of the evil treasure bringeth forth evil things.*
> Matthew 12:35

As your mind becomes renewed to God's truths, by having the Word of God planted deeply in your heart, you will bring forth good things in your life — good words and good actions — which, in turn, will cause you to be "more than a conqueror" through Christ Jesus.

The Law of Sowing and Reaping

If you insulate a house well, you will save money and be more comfortable. If you eat nutritiously and exercise correctly, you will have a strong body, more energy and less sickness. If you pay your tithes, God will bless you financially. If you delight yourself in the Lord, He will give you the desires of your heart (see Psalm 37:4). You "sow" an action and you "reap" a result.

All of life is based on cause and effect, sowing and reaping. The Bible says:

> *Be not deceived; God is not mocked: for whatsoever a man soweth, that shall he also reap. For he that soweth to his flesh shall of the flesh reap corruption; but he that soweth to the Spirit shall of the Spirit reap life everlasting.*
> Galatians 6:7-8

The Renewed Mind and Inner Healing

God's Success Principles

God does not promise you a life without trials, but He has promised you victory in every trial:

> *There hath no temptation taken you but such as is common to man: but God is faithful, who will not suffer you to be tempted above that ye are able; but will with the temptation also make a way to escape, that ye may be able to bear it.* 2 Timothy 2:12

> *If we suffer, we shall also reign with him: if we deny him, he also will deny us.* 1 Corinthians 10:13

God has success principles that apply to every area of your life. His truth, His Word, His principles and His laws will set you free from every bondage, every stronghold, and will produce prosperity in every area of your life.

The Lord instructed Joshua to renew his mind to the Word of God. The Lord spoke to him:

> *This book of the law shall not depart out of thy mouth; but thou shalt meditate therein day and night, that thou mayest observe to do according to all that is written therein: for then thou shalt make thy way prosperous, and then thou shalt have good success.*
> Joshua 1:8

Renewing your mind to God's Word, to His success principles, will cause you to "sow" actions that will "reap" success in every area of your life, including your relationships with God, your family and your friends, as well as success in your job and in your finances.

Your Mind Becomes Conformed to What You Meditate On

You must be careful not to behold or focus on the wrong images, including the wrong image of yourself! You need to be full of the Word, God's truth, His promises, so you won't be overwhelmed by the problems of life. Focus on the promises of God, not the problems, not the mountains in your life.

When necessary, the Holy Spirit will anoint you to glance, not in fear but in faith, at the problems in life. You must look at your problems, your trials, as challenges, as opportunities for God to show His greatness. He has many miracles for you. Reach out by faith and grab them!

Through the mighty power of the Holy Spirit or, negatively, through the power of the enemy, you are transformed into what you meditate on — good or bad, godly or ungodly. Meditating, pondering and reflecting on the Word of God will teach you His principles, His laws, and this will renew your mind. These principles and laws become birthed within you. They will become part of you. Meditation on His Word will cause you to become more and more godlike!

The Word of God states:

> *But we all, with unveiled face, beholding as in a mirror the glory of the Lord, are being transformed into the same image from glory to glory, just as by the Spirit of the Lord.* 2 Corinthians 3:18, NKJ

The Renewed Mind and Inner Healing

If you meditate on the faults of others, you will become like them. If you meditate on the pleasures of the world, you will become like people of the world. If you meditate on the problems in your life instead of on the promises of God's abundant supply (see Philippians 4:19), you will become carnal and fearful in your thinking, and this will block God's miracle-working power in your life.

Praise is a language of faith. Complaining is an attitude, or mind-set, of unbelief and even rebellion. It includes self-pity, and even blaming God! The Lord desires us to praise Him continually for the blessings of life and also for the trials in our lives, and to be set free from such complaining and unbelief! David, said:

> *I will bless the LORD AT ALL TIMES: his praise shall CONTINUALLY be in my mouth.* Psalm 34:1

Some people are willing to praise God *in* their trials, but they can't understand why we should praise God *for* those trials. "Aren't trials caused, directly or indirectly, by the devil?" they might ask. This is true, but God is in control of our lives, and He desires to bring good out of every bad situation. Praising Him for the trials and hardships of life is a language of faith. It shows we trust God, and it "releases" Him to work on our behalf to bring good out of the situation.

Praising for the trial removes fear and enhances our relationship with Him. The Word of God tells us:

> *And we know that all things work together for good to them that love God, to them who are the called according to his purpose.* Romans 8:28

Laugh and Cry Your Way to Freedom

Giving thanks always FOR all things unto God and the Father in the name of our Lord Jesus Christ.
Ephesians 5:20

My brethren, count it all joy when ye fall into divers temptations. James 1:2

Joseph came to know that God brings good out of evil. Years after his brothers sold him into slavery in Egypt, he said to them:

Ye thought evil against me; but God meant it unto good. Genesis 50:20

Over the years, Pattie and I have experienced great blessings from praising God for trials in our lives. For example, our car broke down when we were on our way to a revival meeting in Pittsburgh. Right there on the side of the highway (much to the chagrin of our embarrassed daughter, who hid in the back seat), we danced and praised God FOR THE BREAKDOWN, yes, right there on the side of the road in public.

Within three minutes, an empty car carrier stopped. The driver pulled our car on top and allowed the four of us to squeeze into the cab with him. Then he sped off, taking us to where we could get help, and we arrived on time in Pittsburgh to preach that night. God does all things well.

Once when Pattie was driving in Virginia, a drunk driver hit our car and then left the scene of the accident. Pattie praised God in the dance on the highway, and when I heard of the accident, I also praised God FOR the trial.

The Renewed Mind and Inner Healing

The driver returned to the scene of the accident and paid for our damages.

Last year I was closing a roll-up metal self-storage door and caught three of my fingers in it. When I finally got my fingers out of the door, I was in such terrible pain that I feared permanent damage. With Pattie's strong encouragement, I praised God FOR the accident and the pain. To my amazement, soon the pain vanished, and there was not even a bruise on my fingers, although THE METAL OF THE ACCORDION-LIKE DOOR WAS BENT IN THREE PLACES where my three fingers had been caught!

Trust God and know that He will never let any trial come to you unless He can bring good out of it. Praise God even for the small irritations of life. He will often teach you valuable lessons through them. Murmuring, complaining and self-pity will leave, and a new peace and faith will come into your life.

I encourage you to read Merlin Carothers' book, *Power in Praise,* on the awesome victories and power from praising God for the trials of life.

Adamic Sin and Ungodly Beliefs

Because of Adamic sin and the generational sins of our family line, we live in a world of sin, fear, deception, lies and half-truths. From birth, because of hurts (including negative words and ideas) and rejection by loved ones, our minds have been programmed to a multitude of ungodly beliefs. These wrong beliefs — these incorrect, ungodly ways of thinking — become demonic strongholds in a person's life. Furthermore, they don't just make life more difficult. They squeeze us like an octopus. These strongholds trap us in a spiritual prison of wrong thinking.

Each one of us, to a large extent, lives his life with these wrong beliefs. We believe lies about ourselves, about God, and about others. It is difficult for us to trust God in our hearts when every important person in our lives has let us down, deeply hurt us or disappointed us.

Most people are afraid of and rebel against surrendering their beliefs, ideas and self-control to anyone. This includes God because they assign to God the ungodly qualities of their parents and other authority figures. These wrong beliefs are strongholds and must be broken. Our minds must be renewed to God's way of thinking.

Getting Rid of Ungodly Beliefs

Your mind cannot be "renewed" to God's way of thinking until you are willing to be changed, and until you know how to give up your present ungodly beliefs — your ways of controlling your own life. God wants you totally dependent on Him.

As emphasized throughout this book, one of the major purposes of inner healing and deliverance is to change us on the inside, to produce within us the character of Christ. This includes the mind of Christ — the way He thinks. Therefore, having our minds renewed to God's way of thinking, to His principles and laws, is the most important spiritual tool or principle of inner healing.

The first stage in the renewal of your mind is getting rid of your old ungodly beliefs and ways of thinking, in-

The Renewed Mind and Inner Healing

cluding fears, distrust and rebellion against man and God, and even against change itself. This will prepare you for the next stage in the renewal of your mind, a change to a whole new way of thinking — God's way of thinking, reflecting His truths, His Word, His wisdom, His love.

It will be a life surrendered to God, a life of peace and joy:

> *For the kingdom of God is not meat and drink; but righteousness, and peace, and joy in the Holy Ghost.*
> Romans 14:17

It will be a life of greatly enriched relationships with friends, with loved ones, and with God through the Lord Jesus Christ. I'm sure you want this.

Renewal of the Mind for Physical Healing

With a stressful look on her face, Alicia, a lovely black sister, approached Pattie and me and confided, "I have had migraine headaches for over ten years, and they never leave completely. My head is always in pain and pressure. It makes it hard to be a good mother or wife. Can you help me?"

Thank God, we were able to say that we could help her. We ministered extensively to her for the healing of deep, rage-filled wounds from the past — the root cause of the migraines. Then, in the name of Jesus, we commanded the spirit of migraine to leave permanently. For the first time in years, she was pain-free, healed by the mighty power of God.

Isn't our God wonderful?

Laugh and Cry Your Way to Freedom

We then instructed Alicia in the importance of thanking the Lord repeatedly for His mighty healing miracle in her life. We also had her to repeatedly quote healing scriptures. This is essential to receiving and keeping your miracle. It enables you to believe in your heart that you are healed. Your mind becomes renewed to this truth.

Keeping Your Healing

In the physical healing ministry, one of the greatest lacks in the Body of Christ is the failure to teach Christians how to keep their healing. If you follow certain spiritual principles, you will rarely lose your healing.

When persons are healed and the pains or other symptoms leave, in most cases the devil will bring the symptoms back — to convince them that they are not healed. Your mind needs to be renewed to the important spiritual truth that the return of pains or other symptoms does not mean you have lost your healing. This is a trial of your faith, and you must contend **FERVENTLY** for your healing.

> *For we walk by faith, not by sight.*
> 2 Corinthians 5:7, NKJ

We walk by faith in God's promises, not by what we see or feel. Walking by faith and not by sight is one of the most important principles of faith, and our minds need to be deeply renewed to this principle.

Furthermore, when you are believing for a great miracle in your life, whether for healing, finances, family relationships, open doors of ministry, revival in your church, or

The Renewed Mind and Inner Healing

some other type of miracle, circumstances usually get worse before the miracle comes. You must stand on God's promises and on His faithfulness.

Never focus on your circumstances, nor on what you reason with your natural mind. The miracle will come. The Bible tells us:

And let us not be weary in well doing: for in due season we shall reap, if we faint not. Galatians 6:9

With ten years of nonstop migraines, it would be extremely difficult for Alicia to believe in her heart that she was healed — particularly when she felt the pains returning. Her mind needed to be renewed to the awesome truth that she was, indeed, healed. She needed to be taught how to take authority over any returning migraine pain sent by the devil, and to stand by faith that she was healed. Here are some written instructions we gave to Alicia (and others) so that her mind would be renewed to the truth necessary to keep her healing. Use them to keep your healing too, or even to receive your healing:

1. During the next twenty-four hours, thank God at least twenty-five times for healing you!

Declare to our Lord, "Jesus, I am healed through Your shed blood. I am healed, I am healed! And I thank You, I thank You, I thank You for my healing. Thank You, Jesus." Do this twenty-five times in one day.

2. Command, in the Name of Jesus, any returning pains (or other symptoms) to go, to go, to go.

Get angry at Satan if he tries to put any pain back on you. Jesus took your sickness on the cross. He loves you! You are healed! If even a small amount of pain returns, command it to go. Fight the "good fight of faith."

3. Testify to at least three or four people.

Tell them exactly in detail the healing miracle God has given you. Brag about Jesus!

> *And they overcame him by the blood of the Lamb, and by the word of their testimony.*
> Revelation 12:11

When you have done these three things, if you still have any pain or other symptoms or if you have a serious or long-standing condition such as Alicia had, read out loud the following scriptures three or more times each day (fifty times daily would be much better) for one week:

> *Who his own self bare our sins in his own body on the tree, that we, being dead to sins, should live unto righteousness: by whose stripes ye were healed.*
> 1 Peter 2:24

Repeat many times, "By whose stripes, I was and am healed."

> *Who forgiveth all thine iniquities; who healeth all thy diseases.*
> Psalm 103:3

The Renewed Mind and Inner Healing

Personalize it. Say *"Who healeth all MY diseases."*

Keep praising Jesus for your healing. He is wonderful. He is mighty. He is our Savior, our Healer and our Deliverer. He has healed you.

You have received the healing Jesus purchased for you on the cross at Calvary through His shed blood. He doesn't want you to lose it. The devil will try to steal it from you by bringing back pains or other symptoms to make you think you have lost your healing. Insist on your healing and it will be yours — permanently.

Please feel free to copy the above instructions for "Keeping Your Healing" and make them available for others.

Conclusion

We have described in this book various inner healing methods the Holy Spirit uses to remove from our lives much of the roots of negativity, unbelief, lust, rage, fears and other ungodly ways of thinking. This paves the way for "day and night" meditation on the Word of God to renew our minds deeply to God's victorious ways of thinking and living.

As you become a doer of the Word and live out these truths in everyday life, they will further transform your thinking, your actions and your life. You will have a new and deeper love for God and greatly enhanced relationships with the people around you. You will be freed from the past to live victoriously in every area of your life and to excitedly look forward to the future. You will be *Changed Into His Image Through Inner Healing.*

Chapter 11

Easy Steps to Life-Transforming Inner Healing (and Deliverance)

The previous chapters covered many principles for receiving and ministering inner healing and deliverance. I hope you have found these principles to be exciting, informative and easy to put into practice. EVEN A LITTLE UNDERSTANDING of them will aid you incredibly in being set free and in setting others free as well. I strongly recommend that you review these previous chapters a number of times until the simple principles contained in them become a part of you. Your life will never be the same.

In this chapter I want to summarize these simple principles into steps for inner healing.

There are many layers of hurts in all of our lives, and it would normally take years for them to be removed. But don't be discouraged. You have reason to be excited. Inner healing can come quickly This process can be sped up greatly! Even one or two weeks of fifteen to thirty min-

Easy Steps to Life-Transforming Inner Healing

utes daily of deep self-travail or holy laughter can have life-changing results for you. I will show you how easily this can be done:

Step 1. Make a written list of your major hurts and big disappointments throughout your life, focusing on your childhood years.

Rejection, emotional hurts and abuse from your mother and dad are the most important. I had twenty-one names on my list! List all the people, including religious leaders, who have hurt of disappointed you greatly.

All of us live in much denial, even of the fact that we are in denial! We run from painful truths. We need to face the truth of how greatly our lives have been affected by hurts of the past and cooperate with the Holy Spirit in permitting Him to set us free. Steps two through eight will show you how to be healed from these various hurts on your list.

Step 2. Begin shouting very loudly in tongues in the privacy of your home, or in your automobile.

At home, you can do this either standing up or lying on your face on the floor. I shout in tongues and travail every day while driving in my automobile. Even a few minutes of this shouting will help release your suppressed emotions. Shouting in tongues will often cause a "cleansing" and/or inner healing to take place.

If you do not speak in tongues, see Chapter 3 and the appendix on the baptism in the Holy Spirit. This is a free gift from God, and you don't have to earn it or deserve it. You do have to hunger for it and desire more of God in your life. God has it for you now!

Step 3. Continue shouting in tongues for about two or three minutes until self-travail comes, the *"groanings"* of Romans 8:26!

Shouting in tongues will help you to "open up" to the Holy Spirit so self-travail — sobbing, groaning, crying or even anointed screaming — can more easily begin for the hurts in your life. But you must, in childlike faith, cooperate with the Holy Spirit. He will not force His blessings upon you! As we have seen, such self-travail is the key to rapid, dramatic, life-changing inner healing.

Focus on a deep hurt in your life, rejection or a great disappointment, such as your marriage, your work, your church or your childhood. Then "cooperate" with the Holy Spirit in opening up to self-travail for the healing of your hurt or disappointment.

How do we cooperate with the Lord? You may be thinking, "I don't want it to be in the flesh. If God wants me to scream or to laugh, He will cause it to happen."

The primary cause of Christians being "in the flesh" is our fear of being in the flesh, the fear that we will not be in the Spirit! Because of such fear, we fail to open up to the Holy Spirit as He tries to bring upon us holy laughter, travail, groanings or even screaming! We hold back from prophesying, giving a message in tongues, or delivering a word of knowledge to a friend, pastor or other leader. Fear binds us from cooperating with the Holy Spirit.

Easy Steps to Life-Transforming Inner Healing

Be childlike, be bold, be obedient to the promptings of the Holy Spirit. If you feel sobbing coming, you must yield and start sobbing. If you feel holy laughter coming, then you must start laughing. If you feel a scream could begin, you must yield to it. How? By faith, just start screaming! I do this often!

Don't worry about being in the flesh. In faith, you are cooperating with the Holy Spirit. It will be "in the Spirit"! It will be "anointed"! It will be *"bread"* and not *"a stone"*! You will be blessed awesomely.

If you are at home, keep a pillow handy to cover up your loud travail! I travail almost every day in the automobile, so I don't disturb anyone. Try it. It is an excellent place to travail before the Lord. Jesus said:

> *Verily I say unto you, Except ye be converted, and become as little children, ye shall not enter into the kingdom of heaven.* Matthew 18:3

The Word of God further declares:

> *But God hath chosen the foolish things of the world to confound the wise.* 1 Corinthians 1:27

So don't be afraid to be childlike or to seem foolish to others. Let God have His way!

It is true that self-travail or holy laughter usually comes spontaneously, sovereignly, from God, but the Holy Spirit is always waiting for us to make ourselves available — to cooperate with Him in opening up to an anointing for it. He won't force us to yield to Him. He is kind and patient.

Laugh and Cry Your Way to Freedom

Be childlike. Show your hunger for more of God. By faith, in childlike simplicity, just do it. Laugh, travail, scream! God is going to set you free. The longer it lasts, the more life-transforming your inner healing will be. You may need to repeat this step of moving into self-travail many times in one session of prayer.

Step 4. If self-travail does not come quickly, then ask the Lord for holy laughter for your hurts.

Holy laughter for specific hurts will produce deep inner healing. It will also help you to open up to self-travail. The greater the emotional pain, the more important it is to laugh in the Spirit about it! If your hurt is truly "no laughing matter," then you must laugh long and hard at it!

To help holy laughter flow, to cooperate with the Holy Spirit, do two things:

1. Pray very loudly in tongues — shouting loudly in tongues is best.

2. Then, by faith "prime the pump" with "Hee, hee! Ha, ha! Ho, ho!" about specific hurts in your life. If laughter still hasn't come then try, "Ho, ho! Ha, ha! Hee, hee!" This sounds totally foolish, but as indicated earlier, the Bible does say:

But God hath chosen the foolish things of the world to confound the wise.   1 Corinthians 1:27

Easy Steps to Life-Transforming Inner Healing

These "laughter" words (Ho, ho, ha, ha, hee, hee!) are heavily anointed by the Lord, and are holy words! They will either lead us into deep holy laughter or into self-travail or both! See Chapter 5, "Inner Healing through Holy Laughter."

God wants hunger and childlike humility from us. Cooperate with the Lord. In faith, in expectancy and with your eyes closed, try out a few Hee, hee's, Ha, ha's and ho, ho's for a deep hurt in your life. You may be amazed at what happens!

3. Force yourself to laugh loudly. Be determined that you are going to be set free.

Step 5. In Jesus' name, through spiritual warfare, break the power of generational curses (generational iniquity) unto the third and fourth generation in your family line.

We need to "pray through" until we know we have the victory in every generational area that involves a curse — a negative generational inheritance. With great authority, in the mighty name of Jesus, do spiritual warfare until you feel a witness of the Spirit that the curse is broken. Warfare in English is effective and best at times, but I have found that warfare in tongues is usually dynamically more powerful! Try it. Do it often.

It may take a number of sessions of heavy spiritual warfare to obtain significant victories over generational curses in your family history. For example, I had to break the generational curse of occultism in my life in several different areas of involvement. These included the ouïja board, the "pendulum," visiting a fortune-teller and trying to hypnotize someone. I spent a number of days of much spiritual warfare, including self-travail, to break these curses. Effective prayer is hard work! See Chapter 7, "Breaking the Power of Generational Iniquity."

Step 6. Follow steps two to five above at least two or three times a week for several weeks!

This is of great importance. There are many layers of hurts and many new areas that the Holy Spirit wants to heal. You will need much more inner healing and deliverance.

Step 7. Feed much on the Word of God, the Bible, renewing your mind from being partially negative to being positive.

The Bible tells us that we must meditate on the Word of God day and night — not just occasionally. Read good books and listen to good tapes on faith. Each day, force yourself, discipline yourself, to speak only words of faith, for we walk *"by faith, not by sight"* (2 Corinthians 5:7).

Quote slowly to Jesus from your heart (not just mentally), seven times per day for one week, the following scriptures. As you do, be aware that He is present with you. Tell Him how much you love Him:

> *Nay, in all these things we are more than conquerors through him that loved us.*   Romans 8:37

Easy Steps to Life-Transforming Inner Healing

I can do all things through Christ which strengtheneth me.   Philippians. 4:13

But my God shall supply all your need according to his riches in glory by Christ Jesus.
                                                    Philippians 4:19

Other Special Steps to Follow to Walk in Victory

Here are a few other steps that will ensure victory in your life:

1. Develop a life of praise and worship.

Begin with at least fifteen minutes a day alone with God, just praising and worshipping Him. Sing songs of worship to the Lord Jesus Christ. Much of this praise and worship should be in tongues. Then increase this time to twenty minutes, and then more as you feel the desire — but don't just do it by formulas or legalistic rules.

Make a list of the many blessings in your life — everything good, including His shed blood, your salvation, the baptism in the Holy Spirit, His friendship, your loved ones, your home, your health and your country. Praise Him often for all of these many blessings in your life.

2. Develop a spirit of thanksgiving in place of complaining. Whenever self-pity tries to rise up, begin praising God for the many blessings in your life.

Complaining and self-pity are faith killers. Thanksgiving is a language of faith and appreciation. Only yesterday the Lord showed me that in my heart I was complaining about the large debt I had. Now I must praise God for this trial and for the future victory of becoming debt-free.

3. Be a forgiving person.

Make a habit of praying blessings on those who hurt you. Jesus has instructed us to bless those who curse us and to love our enemies (see Matthew 5:44). The Lord also has commanded us to judge not and condemn not, and to forgive. We must not judge others but bless them in prayer, and sometimes in other ways also. We must be dispensers of blessings, not of instruction or judging. Then we won't be judged or condemned. We will be forgiven! That's good reaping.

4. Repent for any sin in your life, particularly for the sins of negative reactions to hurts and other trials in your life.

This includes the grumbling and complaining about trials in your life, the judging of others, and the desire for revenge. Ask the Lord to search your heart, particularly about judging and criticizing your mother and father and, secondly, your marriage partner.

5. Never, never condemn yourself.

Godly conviction is good, and it brings victorious repentance. Condemnation of oneself brings self-pity, unbelief and spiritual death. Avoid it.

Conclusion

Jesus loves us so greatly. He has taken our pain, our sickness, our fears, our hurts, our rejections, our shame and even our disappointments UPON HIMSELF.

> *Surely he hath borne our griefs, and carried our sorrows.* Isaiah 53:4

Through His shed blood on the cross of Calvary, Jesus has purchased total victory for us in every area of our lives! He has given us the principles to follow to walk in complete victory in life. Inner healing is a free love gift from Him, purchased with His blood. Choose to be free. Don't reject the gift.

DO THIS: FOLLOW EVEN A FEW OF THE SIMPLE GOD-GIVEN PRINCIPLES IN THIS BOOK, and you will be set free to walk in greatly increased joy and intimacy with God and others. You can be released from the hurts, pains and disappointments of life and become an instrument for setting others free. You can become the person God created you to be. Jesus wants to free you to be able to give and receive love, and to enjoy greatly improved relationships with family members, friends, co-workers and with God.

Laugh and Cry Your Way to Freedom, and be *Changed Into His Image Through Inner Healing.*

Appendix

How to Receive the Baptism in the Holy Spirit

How do you receive the baptism in the Holy Spirit, including the accompanying gift of speaking in other tongues? The first step is be sure you are a born-again Christian. Jesus must be living in your heart. This means being "saved." For years I mentally believed in Jesus as my Savior, but He wasn't living in my heart. I was not born again. I didn't even know it was possible to have such an experience — until June 24, 1967, when the Lord Jesus came into my heart!

If you are not sure you are a born-again Christian, ask God, in Jesus' name, to forgive you for the sin in your life. Invite Him to come into your heart. Surrender your life to Him, and you will be born again. You will come to know Jesus personally. Your life will never be the same.

Repeat this prayer:

How to Receive the Baptism in the Holy Spirit

Dear Father God,

In the name of Your Son Jesus, please forgive me for every sin in my life, for every person I have hurt, and for hurting You through my sins and acts of unkindness. I surrender my life to You. Jesus, come into my heart and change me. I receive You, Jesus, as both my Lord and my Savior. I want to live to please You. I surrender my life fully to You.

With your eyes closed, raise your head high and repeat this prayer also:

By faith, Lord Jesus, I see Your precious blood washing over my mind, over my soul, and over my spirit. I thank You that through Your precious blood I am made clean. I am forgiven. I am free of guilt. I am saved. I am born again. I am Your child. Thank You, Lord Jesus.

After praying these prayers one or more times, you will be ready for the next step:

Now You Are Ready to Be Baptized in the Holy Spirit

The baptism in the Holy Spirit, including the powerful manifestation of speaking in tongues, is a free gift from God Himself. It will give you more spiritual power, joy and peace. Also, it will help you walk closer to God. Jesus will become more real to you, and the Bible more exciting. The Lord wants an intimate relationship with you.

No one is worthy of being baptized in the Holy Spirit, and no one can earn it by good works. You need to be childlike and greatly desire this priceless free gift from God, and you need to hunger for more of God in your life. Ask God for it. Asking shows you desire it, that you consider being baptized in the Holy Spirit and speaking in tongues a precious gift.

You receive the baptism in the Holy Spirit by faith — as follows:

(It is extremely helpful to have a Spirit-filled Christian "lay hands" on you as you pray):

1. **Raise your head VERY high, and lift up your hands (with your eyes closed).** This position may be difficult and seem unnatural at first because it makes you feel defenseless. However, it is a powerful way of opening your spirit to God.

2. **With your eyes closed, rapidly speak out loudly (shouting is best) "I love You, Jesus" for about a minute — just one minute.**

Be sure it is very loud. This loudness helps to "open" your spirit to the Lord. It also helps to break an inner vow to be quiet, to suppress one's emotions — a vow most of us have made! (See Chapter 8, "Breaking the Power of Destructive Inner Vows.") When you pray in tongues (or in English), picture Jesus as standing in front of you. He is there, for He said that He would never leave us nor forsake us. Don't pray to the air or to the walls, as I did for years, but pray to God through Jesus. Be aware that He is there in front of you.

How to Receive the Baptism in the Holy Spirit

With this one minute of praise, you will usually begin to feel the presence of the Lord, for God lives in the midst of the praises of His people.

3. After about one minute of shouting "I love You, Jesus," stop English totally.

Then by faith, immediately start speaking words or syllables you don't understand. You can do it. Don't speak one more word of English. But you must open your mouth and speak words you don't understand. Speak these strange sounds, these unknown words, loudly. As you do this, you are beginning to speak in tongues.

The Holy Spirit won't force you to speak in tongues. By faith, you must speak those words. God will give you what you are asking for — the gift of tongues. You may think you are making it up, but those strange sounds are words from God. They are *"bread"* and not *"a stone," "fish"* and not *"a serpent"* (Luke 11:11-13). Keep speaking in tongues for at least fifteen minutes. One or two hours would be better! The longer you speak, the deeper the experience will be.

4. Step out in faith and speak or sing in a second language and then a third.

You can speak or sing in *"divers [many] kinds of tongues"* — not just one (1 Corinthians 12:10). Praying in many new tongues will immensely deepen your experience.

5. Be sure to speak and sing in tongues every day, preferably at least thirty minutes a day.

Your "tongues" will get deeper and deeper. And remember, you can speak in many different tongues.

6. Try shouting in tongues for thirty minutes each day for three days, and see what God will do for you.

From doing this, a sister in Christ moved into a whole new place of intercession. A brother from Ireland reported his prayer life was transformed. A television executive stated, "I am not the same person."

Through the baptism in the Holy Spirit, a door of opportunity has been opened for you to walk in a deeper intimacy with God, to have a greater anointing in your life, and to begin to operate in the gifts of the Holy Spirit. Daily praising, worshipping and interceding in tongues is a supremely important key to walking through that door of opportunity. Expect to see your prayers answered, and more quickly. Remember, pray or sing at least thirty minutes daily in tongues. What a super blessing it is going to be in your life.

Cassette Tape Series by John and Pattie Chappell

Tapes by John Chappell:

1. *Healing the Broken Heart* (6 tapes) $30
2. *Spiritual Warfare* (6 tapes) $30
3. *Ministering to Others* (6 tapes) $30
4. *The Anointing* (6 tapes) $30
5. *How to Receive Your Miracle* (3 tapes) $15
6. *Hearing the Voice of God* (3 tapes) $15
7. *Mistakes in Prayer* (3 90-minute tapes) $15

Tapes by Pattie Chappell:

8. *How to Be Used of God* (6 tapes) $30
9. *Increasing the Anointing in Your Life* (6 tapes) $30

Send me tape set number(s) _____. Include $3.00 shipping and handling for each set.

Please make your checks payable to The Chappell Ministries, Inc. and mail to:

John and Pattie Chappell
The Chappell Ministries, Inc.
P.O. Box 172
Bartow, Florida 33831

(863) 533-6656
E-Mail: JChap777@aol.com

— Notes —

— Notes —

— Notes —

— Notes —

To contact the author for meetings, or for additional books:

John R. Chappell, III
The Chappell Ministries, Inc.
P.O. Box 172
Bartow, FL 33831
(863) 533-6656
e-mail: JChap777@aol.com